The History and Future of Wellness

The History and Future of Wellness

Donald B. Ardell

Kendall/Hunt
Publishing Company
Dubuque, Iowa

Cover art by Kathleen Vande Kleft

Illustrations by Jennifer Jones

Copyright © 1984 Donald B. Ardell

Copyright © 1985 by Kendall/Hunt Publishing Company

Library of Congress Catalog Card Number: 85-80409

ISBN 0-8403-3682-9

Printed in the United States of America
B   403682   01

CONTENTS

FOREWORD

In 1977, Don provided a broad overview of wellness issues and concerns in his book *High Level Wellness: An Alternative to Doctors, Drugs and Disease.* In this new book, Don takes the nation's wellness pulse and tells us the status of wellness in the United States in 1985. He evaluates important social and political contributions to the present wellness movement. In discussing the history of wellness, he identifies the significant breakthrough of events that has been the catalyst for the current wellness movement. He also identifies watershed publications furthering the wellness movement. He discusses the impact special programs have had, and contributions made by research, wellness organizations and special workshops on wellness events.

The second part of Don's book identifies special programs in which wellness is being accomplished in powerful ways in a variety of educational, medical, governmental, community, and industrial settings. In the last two sections of the book, Don discusses important future trends affecting the wellness movement and challenges which we face if the wellness movement is to continue its growth.

Don neglected to include in this book the outstanding and significant contributions that he has made personally to the national wellness movement. His professional expertise, energy, lifestyle, and personal commitments to wellness have been significant factors contributing to the current level of wellness in the United States. Don is a strong promoter of wellness, a very persuasive salesman and certainly one of its foremost advocates. His willingness to spread the wellness message both in person and through his numerous publications is a major force in wellness in the United States today.

In the "Ardell Wellness Report," Don says "wellness is too serious to be presented grimly." He lives up to this attitude in this book. His exuberant enthusiasm and excitement for wellness are contagious. His message is presented in a lively, exciting fashion. One cannot leave this book without being further committed to a wellness lifestyle.

Fred Leafgren, Ph.D., Assistant Chancellor
University of Wisconsin, Stevens Point

ACKNOWLEDGMENTS

To all the quoted participants at wellness conferences who filled out the questionnaires, the experts who responded to phone interviews, and the pros involved in diverse aspects of the wellness business who volunteered their opinions about where we have been, where we are, and where we are headed.

To Michael Samuelson, Tom Connellan, and others at the National Center for Health Promotion in Ann Arbor, Michigan for their support in general and in particular for the widespread distribution of the earlier, abridged version of this work.

To Mark Crooks of Kansas City—excellent feedback on the earlier edition.

To Russ Kisby and PARTICIPaction in Toronto—for artwork that inspired many of the drawings in this edition.

INTRODUCTION

"Wellness" has gone from being a confused term associated with "pop psychology" and "fringe elements" to being described by Newsweek magazine as an "inalienable right" of all Americans. The Auto Workers Union has mandated in their contract with General Motors that "wellness" benefits be provided for all members. Major employers such as Levi Strauss, Tenneco, IBM, PepsiCo. and Johnson & Johnson have spent, and continue to spend, hundreds of thousands of dollars to ensure the "wellness" of their employees.

What fills in the space between obscurity and acceptance? What transpired during the past ten–fifteen years which has resulted in conservative business giants recognizing the need to supplement "nose to the grindstone" with "running shoes to the track"? The answers to those questions form the basis of this book.

Don Ardell has been a major contributing force behind the removal of quotation marks from the word wellness. I invite you to explore *The History and Future of Wellness* comfortable in the knowledge that these are merely the opening chapters in the growing awareness movement supporting the need for lifestyle enhancement or WELLNESS.

by Michael Samuelson
Executive Vice President
The National Center For Health Promotion

The History and Future of Wellness

ONE
A Brief Background

A Movement And/Or A Fad?

One of the most often-heard questions at wellness meetings is whether the current activity and interest in wellness is a fad. Another common question is whether wellness endeavors should be considered a "movement" at this time. Both questions are arguable, although the utility of time so spent is marginal.

A check of several dictionaries[5] suggests that wellness clearly is a movement. The word movement means "a change in position," or "activities of a group toward the achievement of a goal." No need to belabor that the range of wellness efforts are directed at shifting away from the status quo medical system and toward the realization of advanced health status. This reflects a changed position and concerted, goal-directed endeavors. Wellness is a movement.

What does the wellness movement have in common with hoola hoops, pet rocks, Rubic cubes, Cabbage Patch Dolls, and the like? The dictionaries offer the following regarding a fad: "A practice or interest followed for a time with exaggerated zeal," or "a fashion taken up with great enthusiasm for a brief period, a craze." (In case you are curious, a "craze" is defined as a "great but short-lived enthusiasm for something.")

There are three elements of interest in these specifications of a fad. One is the lack of any negative connotation attached to the idea; another is the focus on the temporary quality of the phenomenon; the third is the attention to zeal or high energy commitment that characterizes all fads. What shall we make of all this. *Is* wellness a fad?

At one time, the question offended me. Associating hoola hoops and the like with a philosophy that celebrates personal responsibility, a balanced lifestyle, environmental awareness, spiritual growth, and so much that reflects a deliberate and thoughtful quest for personal advancement seemed ludicrous, irreverent, and otherwise inappropriate. It *still* does; however, there is no point of any concern as to whether wellness does or does not have fad characteristics. What is wrong with "exaggerated zeal," or "great enthusiasm" if the object of said passion is noble?

However, there is not much to be said for the "brief period"/"for a time" aspect. In that regard, we all have an interest as individuals and as a society

1

in the continuance of the wellness movement as a permanent fashion and cultural commitment.

Strictly speaking, wellness *is* a movement but is *not* a fad. But such a debate is of little value. A more pressing inquiry concerns the impact of what wellness is and what it can become.

The Current Status of the Wellness Movement

Wellness is a growth industry. It is expanding exponentially. The state of the art is vastly better than it was in Halbert L. Dunn's time, or even in 1977 when *High Level Wellness: An Alternative to Doctors, Drugs, and Disease* was published. The Assistant Surgeon General, William Foege, observes:

> *An important weapon against new health risks is the growing interest of the American people in wellness.* Prevention in the 1970s must include teaching people how they can become part of the health team by determining their own healthy destiny.[6]

Those of us close to the scene know that the present state of the movement is promising but also that we have a long way to go. Most companies still have no wellness programs. Most hospitals have programs in name only. Most schools have nothing remotely similar to wellness programs. Most doctors do not encourage their patients to learn wellness skills (though there are more exceptions to this rule than ever before). And neither the Congress nor the Administration gives consideration to the wellness-related consequences of public policies which affect both personal health and national well being.

The constituents of wellness programs, the sponsors of wellness centers, the participants of wellness conferences, and the practitioners of wellness lifestyles are mainly white, middle class, well-educated, and basically "healthy" people. In other words, the status quo regarding the impact of the wellness movement is limited. Fortunately, the trend line is promising.

This situation, a great trend line but a limited reality, gives a double message. It suggests that the history and future of wellness is good and not so good, which is a difficult position to reconcile. It invites recall of F. Scott Fitzgerald's line that "the test of a first-rate intelligence is the ability to hold two opposed ideas in the mind at the same time, and still retain the ability to function."

Let us examine the events which created the promising trend line, the major elements of the wellness movement, and the issues to be addressed if it is to extend beyond the advantaged segment of our population.

What is Wellness?

Wellness is a conscious and deliberate approach to an advanced state of physical and psychological/spiritual health. This is a dynamic or ever-changing, fluctuating state of being. Even the self-actualized, transformational types who chant and attend all wellness conferences have their bad moments. They just do not dwell in the pits or lurk overlong in the Slough of Despond.

Wellness has the following characteristics, as defined by this writer and many others:

- A balanced approach. There is much more to wellness than just being fit. Five commonly employed areas or dimensions of wellness are self-responsibility, nutritional awareness, stress awareness and management, physical fitness, and environmental sensitivity. Another way to organize the major elements of wellness-oriented life is along six dimensions, as is done at the University of Wisconsin–Stevens Point Institute for Lifestyle Improvement:[8] social, emotional, spiritual, physical, occupational, and intellectual. Yet another often-used model at the Human Resources Institute[9] employs a different set of dimensions: safety and use of medical resources; tobacco, alcohol, and drug usage; nutrition and weight control; exercise and physical fitness; stress and stress management; human relations, self development, and community involvement.

- A positive and fun approach. The motive force behind wellness lifestyles is near-term, attractive payoffs and benefits. Living this way is considered a richer way to be alive. If this lifestyle did nothing to minimize illness or prolong life, it would be worthwhile as it improves the quality of existence and the satisfaction of being. Fortunately, it almost surely has favorable prospects for reduced morbidity and mortality.

- A systematic approach. There is a strong belief among wellness promoters that giving information is not enough; even if such information is interesting, inspirational and motivational, positive, and balanced. People need more; specifically, they need a way to get started that will carry them successfully through the early period of behavior change maintenance. In wellness, this means an eight week personal wellness plan having at least the following six elements:

1. Written goal statements that are positive, measurable, and have a time period.

2. Written goal supportive activity commitments that insure action in support of each goal.

3. A listing of payoffs and barriers, which clarifies and strengthens motivation and identifies likely difficulties and means for overcoming said obstacles.

4. A written contract to complete the plan, witnessed by friends, associates, and supporters.

3

5. A set of benchmarks with which to chart progress.

6. A method or technique of some kind to evaluate and revise the wellness plan.

The other ingredient in wellness programs is attention to the impact of norms, expectations, and other cultural factors on lifestyle patterns. It is extremely difficult to develop and/or continue a conscious commitment to wellness if one receives no encouragement or support of any kind at home or work for such efforts; it is even more difficult if the environments of which one is a part are hostile or otherwise injurious to good health practices.

These are aspects of wellness which are found in the most highly developed of the thousand-plus corporate, hospital, and free-standing centers. The emphasis varies, of course, but an appreciation of this underlying ethic will help to distinguish wellness from related programs, especially health promotion, health education, holistic health, and medical self care.

Briefly, the main features of these endeavors are as follows:

- Health Promotion. Of all the phrases listed above, including wellness, health promotion is the most popular term in use today. It refers to a broad variety of activities and services, including risk reduction classes (e.g., weight loss and stop smoking clinics), testing, health hazard assessments, jogging and other fitness activities, physical exams, and so on. Health promotion is a broad category, distinguished from the term wellness because it is not focused exclusively on health enhancement. It is an umbrella term that covers risk reduction activities (e.g., blood pressure control procedures) and wellness endeavors (e.g., aerobics dance classes).

- Health Education. This has been around longer than any of the terms mentioned here, and is popular in most graduate schools. The focus has been on risk reduction and problem amelioration through retraining of attitudes and behaviors. Another specialization has been on patient education, that is, helping people with medical concerns and problems to better cope and function. Unlike health promotion, health education has not been geared to achieving higher levels of health beyond the absence of illness and disease. Health education has few of the qualities listed as the essence of wellness programming.

- Holistic Health. Advocates of holistic health and programs bearing the term emphasize the idea of mind/body connections in health and illness, personal responsibility, and a balanced lifestyle. An integration of many aspects of optimal functioning, especially fitness, nutrition, and stress management, are important components of this approach. The special orientation of holistic practices and programs, however, is on the treatment of illness conditions. Modalities, therapies, and varied

4

forms of treatment of a *non-drug, non-surgical* nature are emphasized.

- Medical self-care. As the name suggests, this orientation promotes personal responsibility for health by teaching appropriate levels of self sufficiency—such as by being your own doctor, sometimes. Many consider a knowledge of self care skills a basic ingredient in personal responsibility, and a giant step toward a commitment to a wellness lifestyle.

It should be clear that these five areas are highly interconnected and supportive of common objectives. All that varies is the emphasis. Distinctions are arbitrary and often inapplicable; definitions are not universally shared. It makes good sense, therefore, to look beyond the labels to actual program content to recognize the true nature of what a given institution offers.

Shaping Events

Why did wellness programs begin to appear in the late 1970s and not earlier? What events, factors, or other conditions created a climate conducive to the spread of such a departure idea from the prevailing health system status quo? In other words, what caused the paradigm shift at this particular point in time?

Drawing on the opinions of the experts surveyed, and the contributions of hundreds who responded to evaluation forms inviting audience feedback and commentaries on the same questions, ten major developmental factors can be identified. Without most of these factors, few if any of the wellness events would have occurred.

Dr. Robert Thompson, Medical Director of Group Health Cooperative of Puget Sound in Seattle, Washington, helped place these events in perspective when he wrote:

> In response to your request for my thoughts on the wellness movement and its history, I offer the following: I believe one of the earliest events of significance in the wellness movement occurred when one of our ancestors crawled from the primordial ocean onto dry land to avoid being eaten. I'm a bit vague on some historical events after this until more modern times.

Restricting this analysis to "more modern times," it is possible to make matters just a little less vague by discussing ten factors and trends that shaped the climate for and nature of the wellness movement. These are:

1. Breakthrough Works

2. Cost Crisis

3. Consumer Consciousness

4. Mind/Body Awareness

5. Horrible Good Things

6. Industry Responsiveness/Initiatives

7. Powerful Individual Voices

8. Other Movements

9. Research

10. Organizations

Of course, these factors and events did not occur in isolation: nearly everything that happens is related to something else. In fact, I believe these factors were so closely identified as to deserve a new word, or "sniglet" as it would be called on the tv comedy show "Not Necessarily The News." The sniglet nominated to capture this phenomenon is "inextricably intertwinked."

Breakthrough Works

Six deserve recognition, none more so than a publication released by the Canadian Ministry of Health and Welfare in 1974 entitled *A New Perspective on the Health of Canadians*.[10] This was an extraordinary document; it presented the epidemiological evidence for the significance of lifestyle and environmental factors on health or sickness. *A New Perspective . . .* gave us the "health field concept;" contained a call for a score of national health promotion strategies; and presented persuasive evidence that health status advances and lowered personal and societal medical bills would come about only when Canadians began to assume more responsibility for their own health. It was filled with fascinating quotes, references, and examples, and was unlike anything else up to that time in its forthright challenge to the prevailing medical approach to dealing with health hazards. It was highly influential in persuading numerous American medical leaders to rethink current assumptions based upon high technology, treatment focused medicine; tens of thousands of the Report was distributed throughout the United States. Unfortunately, it was ignored in Canada.[11] Anyone involved in a professional sense in wellness promotions should be familiar with this landmark work.

Another breakthrough was the release by the *Senate Select Committee on Nutrition and Human Needs* of a report on dietary goals for the United States.[12] (The Chairman and chief promoter of the report was Senator George McGovern.) This document showed the link between diet and disease, based on expert testimonies before, and research studies on behalf of, the Senate Committee. The Report contained a call for sweeping changes in American food consumption patterns. The recommendations for far less salt, sugar, meat, and dairy products produced a great outcry from the affected industries. Though subsequent Select Committee Reports were watered down, and the

Select Committee itself stripped of powers and funds due to the lobbying of the food industry, the "damage" was done or, more accurately for wellness purposes, the value was rendered. *Dietary Goals . . .* is still widely quoted and referenced.

A third breakthrough work was the American Hospital Association's Policy Statement on the "Hospital's Responsibility for Health Promotion," adopted by the Board of Trustees of the AHA at its Annual Meeting in 1979.[13] This legitimized, sanctioned, and encouraged a development already underway: the establishment of health promotion and wellness centers by a small number of American hospitals. Again, anyone involved in a hospital-related wellness program should be familiar with the language of this statement, a declaration of unwavering dedication to a role judged to be at the top of the progressive institution's mission.

A fourth landmark development was the release in 1979 by the outgoing Secretary of what was then the Department of Health, Education and Welfare of a document entitled *Healthy People*.[14] This was the American version of *A New Perspective. . . .* It contained a ringing endorsement of the need for a shift away from public and governmental support of high technology, doctor-led, hospital-centered treatment medicine in favor of lifestyle and environment strategies by which we could avoid so many illnesses in the first place.

The fifth breakthrough was the "Stay Well Plan" designed by Blue Shield of Northern California for the Mendocino School District.[15] Seeking a way to control rising health insurance rates and to motivate employees to make an effort to avoid unnecessary use of medical care, a first-of-its-kind innovation was set up by the School District with Blue Shield's support. Medical self-care and classes in risk reduction, exercise, and other such topics were offered to the employees, along with an attractive incentive. The incentive was the "stay well" reward: use less than $500. in medical care in any given year, and receive (in a retirement account) whatever is left. If no medical utilization occurs, there are no charges and the employee gets a full $500. rebate. The plan has been very successful. The school district has saved $250 thousand dollars in premiums (and it is a small school district; the potential saving for large corporations is awesome), the interest earned on employee "nest eggs" has purchased several school buses. Insurance premiums which cost $105. a month per employee in 1978 when the program began, now cost $63. a month despite rate increases nearly everywhere else at around 18 percent annually.[16] Most important, the Stay Well Program is being tested on a trial basis in more than 100 major corporations throughout the United States. Keep in mind that this breakthrough idea did *not* shape or reflect the budding wellness movement at the time of its conception or implementation. What it has done is give business leaders a strategy leading to the expansion of wellness programming in years to come. Do not be surprised if a variation of this approach is soon a standard benefit option. After all, why shouldn't workers who take good care of themselves and use less medical care derive some financial payoff for doing so?

The sixth and last of the breakthrough works was the publication in 1975–76 of two documents, both a collection of speeches and essays commissioned by the most influential of American foundations entitled *Doing Better and Feeling Worse*[17] and *Future Directions in Health Care*.[18] Together, these two books contained 42 articles by the leading lights of the medical establishment, and most of them expressed in their own way the idea that ". . . things have gone awry and that only substantial reforms will set them right." Both are still available from the foundations and other sponsoring organizations involved in their development. As with the above noted breakthrough works, both documents deserve the attention of anyone seeking to understand how the environment for wellness was cultivated and shaped.

Cost Crisis

The rate of annual increases in health care spending, the total dollars involved, the percent of GNP consumed by this sector of the economy (10.8), and the individual burden of these figures on American consumers regarding out-of-pocket and health insurance charges: all these cost aspects have combined to create a great interest in new and different ways to control medical bills.[19] This has been especially influential at the corporate level, where rising medical insurance benefit payments (currently at $80 billion annually) cut into profits and lead to increases in the costs of doing business. The desperate need for something which would lessen the demand and need for economy-ruining medical care charges fueled interest in the emerging wellness movement.

Jerry Miller of the Health Insurance Association of America replied for himself and James Moorefield concerning the constructive effect of rising costs on the responsiveness of business to wellness:

> The explosive rise of health care costs in the 1970s gave momentum to many reforms from many different directions. Indeed, concern with the rising cost of health benefit plans has sparked increasing interest and involvement by employers in worksite wellness programs, spreading from top management to all levels of employees.

Sharon Yenney, a former Vice-President of the American Hospital Association, saw the cost crunch as a plus for wellness:

> Another positive force is the high cost of medical technology and the potential bankruptcy of long illnesses. If cures were easy and life could be sustained inexpensively, health promotion would not enjoy the popularity that it has today. Financial motivation can be powerful. High costs have been a key issue in getting businesses involved in providing programs for their employees and their families and the trend of worksite health promotion programs holds great potential for the movement.

8

Consumer Consciousness

Throughout the last decade, changes have taken place in the willingness of citizens to inform themselves about a range of issues, including ways to care for their own minor medical needs. Dr. Tom Ferguson, editor of Medical Self Care, calls this public interest in self treatment "the third wave in health,"[20] a reference to Alvin Toffler's book on the subject of where we are heading and what we are likely to be doing there.[21] Related to this self-care element is a health information explosion—a media fascination with the topic. Also mentioned in this context by several of the respondents was an increasing disenchantment with materialism and the depersonalization of society, coupled with a search for meaning and personal fulfillment. The wellness philosophy encourages the individual to explore values and purposes as essential and rewarding elements of personal wellness planning.

Cecilia Runkle and Wendy Squires at the Kaiser Permanente Medical Group in Oakland put it this way:

> Consumers are choosing to be more active in decision-making. They are more involved in services heretofore carried out by professionals: home and car repair, quality control of products, and medical self-care.

Once again, Dr. Robert Thompson demonstrated an original and figurative way of expressing the idea that the medical care establishment overspecialized and overtechnologized.

> . . . to the extent that people felt increasingly uneasy with the idea of their eyeballs going there, their ears going there, their right big toe going still a third place with the resulting loss of humanism in the whole transaction as increasingly high technology was attempted to be substituted for good basic communication. At the present time, I believe there is a swing back in the other direction, since about the mid 1960s.

Mind/Body Awareness

Wellness programs have a twin focus: physical *and* psychological wellbeing. If the latter were not a key part of the concept, far fewer hospitals (especially sectarian institutions) and spiritually-oriented individual promoters[22] would have been interested, and consequently less would have been heard about the wellness idea. The stage was set for this receptivity throughout the sixties and seventies, and may have reached its zenith with the literature concerning the role of mental states and intentions or will in overcoming disease. The best known example of this factor might be the book *Anatomy Of An Illness* by Norman Cousins.[23] The mind-body awareness interest was (and remains) at the core of other, equally powerful social forces, especially the highly influential self actualization ideas (Abraham Maslow,[24] Carl Rogers[25] and the literature on the lessons of Eastern philosophies (Alan Watts,[26] George Leonard,[27] Fritjof Capra[28]).

9

Horrible Good Things

This deliberate oxymoron refers to the much-cited "benefits" that resulted from or at least were encouraged by the mistakes, deceits, abuses, and other perturbations of the last decade. Specifically, several experts cited Vietnam, the over-specialization and technologizing of health care, the epidemic levels of coronary disease, the decline of organized religion, the threatened breakup of the American family, and the growing sense of geographic fragmentation as factors in the rise of desirable counter trends. Examples of such positive reactions would be a greater willingness on the part of "ordinary" Americans to question authority figures (i.e., doctors); a desire for personal services ("touch" and caring in medicine); a search for ways to reduce one's chances of suffering premature chronic disease; and a desire for holistic alternatives that have encouraged participation and personal involvement.

Mary Beth Love saw the same factors and concluded that the best aspect of the attendant constructive backlash was "the demystification of all professionals."

Carl Yordy, Senior Program Officer at the National Academy of Sciences, Institute of Medicine, wrote:

> Whatever its roots, the wellness phenomenon is very real. I believe there are aspects of these attitude changes similar to organized religion. This last impression is strengthened every time I read a brochure advertising a holistic health conference.

Dr. Thomas Vogt at the Portland Health Services Research Center of the Kaiser Permanente Medical Care Program addressed the idea of "scientific rationalism gone amok" in an insightful and thorough manner. His observations merit reproduction in full:

> The most important event in the history of this "movement" was the rise of scientific rationalism in the eighteenth and nineteenth centuries. Prior to that time medicine was not terribly effective, but it was wellness oriented, and tended to see the human condition as a gestalt. It was, after all, the Greeks who originated the idea of a "healthy mind in a healthy body." Because the reductionism of science worked so effectively against the major infectious diseases, and because rising populations had made these conditions an almost inevitable consequence of life, medicine forgot its roots, lost sight of the fact that illness is a resultant vector between level of exposure, type of exposure, and degree of resistance. Public health successes of the late nineteenth century (not so much medical ones) produced a revolutionary change in the expectation that mankind was fated to die early of contagious diseases. It also produced the notion that public health and well-being were not personal responsibilities, but rather were the responsibility of public agencies. Thus, the short term benefits were accompanied by some rather drastic long-term consequences. . . .

Industry Responsiveness/Initiatives

In 1977, United States companies were paying an average of $1,250. annually per employee for all health related costs, or a total of $33 billion. According to the U.S. Chamber of Commerce, the figures today are $2,500. plus and $80. billion, respectively. Health costs constitute six percent of company payrolls; many firms are facing thirty to forty percent health insurance rate hikes this coming year. Mary Longe at the Center for Health Promotion of the American Hospital Association stated that a belief in wellness as a cost containment strategy is the overriding reason for corporate enthusiasm and support for both business and hospital wellness activities. Other motives frequently mentioned are to reduce absenteeism and high turnover, to bolster the corporate image, and to improve employee morale. The openness of corporate managers to the idea of worksite health promotion and wellness was also sparked by evidence from studies by the U.S. Chamber of Commerce[29] and other industrial groups which established a link between company and employee health levels.[30] More recently, the business community has been hearing from some of its own leadership that the linkage extends even wider to encompass community well-being.[31] Thus, the truly healthy company is one operated by healthy workers who live in a healthy community. At least this is the position of the most innovative in responding to the cost containment challenge by establishing landmark programs during the early 1980s. Among the better corporate examples of such a trend are Metropolitan Life, Safeco, Sentry Insurance, Bonnie Bell, Kimberly Clark, Control Data, Western Federal Savings and Loan, IBM, Xerox, Johnson and Johnson, Pepsico, Abt Associates, Chase Manhattan Bank, Prudential Insurance, Hubbard Milling, Canada Life Assurance, Scherer Lumber, General Foods, Shaklee, National Semiconductor, Lockheed Missiles and Space, and Tenneco, to name a few.[32]

At the start of 1985, more than 50,000 U.S. firms and 1,000 Canadian companies were involved in some aspect of worksite health promotion. One survey (Cox, M. H., *Journal of Cardiac Rehabilitation,* 4 (4), 1984, p. 136) reported four major reasons for the strong level of business support for health promotion: (1) a shift toward self-fulfillment as a work value; (2) belief in the illness-reduction qualities of fitness programs; (3) the apparent connection between health promotion and improved health, attitudes, and attendance records of worksite participants; and (4) an aging workforce, more appreciative of the benefits of personal health initiatives.

Powerful Individual Voices

Throughout the 1970s, books appeared which attracted a large following and influenced the thinking of millions, including nearly everyone who would later play a role in wellness programming. Looking at all the major topic categories, several writers spring to mind as crucial players in setting the stage for the wellness movement, which would later integrate many aspects of their teachings. Readers as yet unfamiliar with these extraordinary contributions are encouraged to examine each book mentioned; their contents remain invaluable and the major contentions in each provide insights on still-existing issues.

- Self Responsibility. Ivan Illich's *Medical Nemesis*[33] heads the list. Also notable are Rick Carlson's *End of Medicine*,[34] Robert Mendelsohn's *Confessions Of A Medical Heretic*,[35] Rene Dubois' *Mirage of Health*,[36] and Harry Browne's *How I Found Freedom In An Unfree World*.[37]

- Nutritional Awareness. Nathan Pritikin's[38] books head this list. Included on it must be Frances Moore Lappe's *Diet for a Small Planet*[39] and Emmanuel Cheraskin's *Psychodietetics* and *Diet and Disease*.[40]

- Physical Fitness. At the top of this honor roll would be Kenneth Cooper's *Aerobics* family of books,[41] followed by George Sheehan's[42] running books and Covert Bailey's *Fit or Fat*.[43]

- Stress Awareness and Management. Hans Selye's *Stress Without Distress*,[44] Herbert Benson's *The Relaxation Response*,[45] and Kenneth Pelletier's *Mind As Healer, Mind As Slayer*,[46] were the most influential in the late 1970s in generating an awareness of, and a capacity for, responding to the inescapable realities of daily stress and thereby preparing readers for the bigger picture. Namely, wellness.

- Medical Self Care. Donald Vickery's *Lifeplan For Your Health* and *Take Care of Yourself: A Consumer's Guide to Medical Care* (with James Fries),[47] Michael Samuels and Hal Bennett's *The Well Body Book*,[48] Keith Sehnert's *How To Be Your Own Doctor (Sometimes)*,[49] Tom Ferguson's *Medical Self Care Magazine*,[50] and Donald Kemper (et.al.) *The Healthwise Handbook*.[51]

Other Movements

The wellness concept has benefited from the growth and development of other movements. Individuals initially attracted by some of the following issues developed interests, concerns, skills, and commitments which often made them highly responsive and committed to wellness approaches. The experts mentioned nine topical areas which in themselves represent movements, all compatible and consistent with wellness and supportive of its purposes. These major factors are holistic health, the womens' movement (which placed a major emphasis on health care and system reform), consciousness-raising and personal effectiveness trainings (EST, Actualizations, Arica, LifeSpring, etc.), ecology interests, the running boom, aerobic dance classes, futurism, and health and/or natural food groups.

Such a list is not exhaustive; other movements addressed quality-of-life concerns. The main point is that wellness did not spring unaided out of nowhere. Instead, it was a logical next step in seeking to create healthier, balanced, and integrated lifestyles and communities.

Research

More and better data on the impact of lifestyles has been available in recent years. This has been invaluable for managers and others who need plausible evidence to support wellness investment recommendations. Jerry Miller cited the "evolution of vastly more sophisticated health promotion strategies, drawing increasingly upon the behavioral sciences and interdisciplinary approaches" as crucial in permitting the present level of wellness programming." Miller added that the quality of current evidence is "a far cry from the personal hygiene class of a generation or so ago."

The specific research projects which seem to stand out as most influential in demonstrating the extraordinary consequences of personal behaviors on health status are:

1. The Belloc and Breslow longitudinal study showing the impact of seven simple behaviors on life expectancy and morbidity levels.[52]

2. The Paffenbarger reports on longshoremen and Harvard Alumni, again demonstrating the high payoffs of exercise and similar habit patterns.[53]

3. The Framingham studies on risk factors of heart disease, leading to the development of an evidentiary base for the popular health hazard appraisal instruments.[54]

4. The development, testing, and refinement of the health hazard appraisal by Lew Robbins at Methodist Hospital in Indianapolis, Indiana.

5. The Surgeon General's Report on Smoking and Health[55] and the years of research and testing that led to it, marking the beginning of the time when links between smoking and varied diseases were incontrovertible (except to tobacco interests) and enabling later legislative efforts to control tobacco sales and advertising.

Years before these six (and numerous other) research and health education endeavors were even initiated, another fundamental knowledge base was developed. This material, gathered by Leon Kass,[56] Thomas McKeown,[57] Victor Fuchs,[58] and many others,[59] showed that major health status advances since the turn of the century were due far more to environmental improvements than either medical technologies or immunological breakthroughs, as commonly assumed. Many of the respondents to this wellness survey properly noted this research breakthrough as a fundamental step, a necessary cognitive recognition, enabling support in later years for a wellness movement. Among those who did so was Dr. Donald R. Griffith of the Midelfort Clinic in Eau Claire, Wisconsin.

One of the biggest advances in past decades has been the conquest of infectious disease. No longer in most parts of the world do we have epidemics or large areas of endemic infectious disease which sweep away populations. The result has been a state of general health previously unknown in history.

Organizations

Influential individuals, other movements, crises of one kind or another, great books, and research advances were all part of the overall thrust of events and factors leading to current public responsiveness to and initiatives for what we call a wellness movement. But there was at least one other element in this complex equation—and that was the activities of certain professional organizations. Through conferences, special committees, and especially lifestyle programming for their own professionals and the constituents they serve, several organizations helped further the interest in healthier lifestyles—and the wellness movement that grew from such activities. Four seem to stand out in this respect: the President's Council on Physical Fitness and Sports (in business for 26 years!), the Society for Prospective Medicine, the Association for Fitness in Business, and YMCA's throughout the land. All could have done a lot more (especially the latter three), others did a little something here and there (e.g., the American Health Planning Association), but most did nothing (e.g., The American Medical Association, The American Public Health Association). All things considered, the four made positive contributions in the early years which helped prepare a better climate for wellness and some, like the Association for Fitness in Business (AFB), will probably be leading agents in wellness promotion in the coming years. (The AFB has grown from 25 members in 1975 to over 3000 today—many of these members are wellness directors or otherwise employed in the broader health promotion (rather than narrow fitness) field.

Expert Opinions

A number of experts suggested factors which did not fit any of the ten categories.

For example, Irwin Wolkstein of the Washington, D.C. Health Policy Alternatives Group wrote:

> A date of significance was marked by the government taking on the tobacco issue. Another important action was in auto safety and the 55 mile

speed limit, although the latter was related to energy conservation as well. A third action of note was the fluoridation of water.

Mary Longe of the American Hospital Association noted another favorite influence on the movement:

> Networking among wellness professionals. True in most emerging fields, but extraordinarily characteristic in the wellness movement.

Dr. Ken Cooper of "aerobics" fame and Executive Director of The Cooper Clinic in Dallas, Texas had this to offer:

> . . . the publicity and television coverage of running, including Frank Shorter's 1972 gold medal in the Olympic Marathon. Also, the accomplishments of Mark Spitz in the Olympics.

In characteristic independent fashion, Dr. George Sheehan refused to be boxed in about any particular shaping event:

> I suspect that wellness movements are an after-the-fact synthesis of a grass roots movement back to the body. The seed has been in the common people. Some experts have stamped on it—others have watered it—I doubt that anything can stop it.

Larry Chapman, head of Health Promotion Associates in Seattle, Washington, expressed a belief that might qualify under the "consumer consciousness" heading, yet seems somewhat apart:

> Wellness is a manifestation of a social response to a perception of powerlessness . . . an increasing need to feel good about something, an 'internality' toward the quality of life issues. In short, a key event or development in the shaping of an openness to wellness was the overly complex nature of life in our times leading to a classic 'high tech vs. high touch' conflict.

George Leonard felt that the influence of the Esalen Institute at Big Sur, California, should not be overlooked:

> All the major ideas that emerged and gained a foothold in the seventies and eighties were brought up, refined, and promoted at Esalen in the sixties.

Finally, the observations of Dr. Robert Bertera, Health Promotion Coordinator at Dupont De Nemours and Company in Wilmington, Delaware provides yet another way of seeing how the movement was indirectly shaped and affected:

> The increased availability of trained professionals concerned about health and lifestyle (i.e., health educators, nutritionists, fitness instructors, family practice physicians, nurse practitioners, occupational and community-based physicians and nurses, etc.). The improving quality of resource material available from voluntary health agencies (e.g., Freedom from Smoking in 20 Days by the American Lung Association; or Breast

15

Self-Exam Slide-Tape by the American Cancer Society) and from commercial vendors and production companies.

Jim Mayr, a good friend and a physician who has been encouraging wellness throughout his varied career, offered something of an international perspective. Dr. Mayr's comments reflect his special knowledge of German history and culture—and his frustrations with the slow pace of the wellness movement in his home town of Milwaukee.

> Don, I'd like to offer a bit of historical perspective, in regard to the Wellness Movement. Are you familiar with the German "Turnverein" or Turners? Although the concept goes far back in German history, the movement actually got its modern start in Germany under Napoleonic French occupation. It was a combination nationalistic, social, economic and personal development support group. It became quite popular in the German-settled Midwest, as a center for gymnastic and related sports events, personal health development . . . such as encouragement of hiking, love of nature (Liebe für die Natur), swimming and the like, and the discouragement of smoking, excessive drinking, etc. In many ways, the Turners embraced much of what is now advocated under "Wellness." With the enterance of the US in WW I, the entire movement came to an abrupt end. Active ridicule for healthy habits became the norm, and rather strongly survives in my native city of Milwaukee today. (Also, my occasionally negative or pessimistic outlook on life, was probably a 3 generation-removed reaction.)
>
> Here, the norm is the beer gut and the Friday fish fry. Only upidy people jog . . . or those university types. I would guess that the average Milwaukean is at least 30 pounds over a Utah or California counterpart. (Myself included, despite the daily swim . . . I could cry.)
>
> Also at present, many in this area are undergoing strong economic reversals . . . many highly-paid, but relatively unskilled, union jobs are gone forever. These folks are not supportive of wellness.
>
> I find this quite curious, as when I was an exchange student in Austria and West Germany, both utterly defeated in WW II, there was still much general support for the old "Gesundheit" health activities. Everybody takes a daily walk. Many do love their beer, but they still underweigh their Wisconsin counterparts.

The above analysis is my own way of cataloging and interpreting events based on a reading of the literature and involvement in the movement, supplemented by the observations of the experts polled by mail. Of equal value and interest are the thousand or so responses to a participant survey form distributed at the three major wellness conferences previously noted.

Wellness Conference Participant Opinions

The first question on the survey was: "What do you consider the five most important factors which have affected the climate for wellness and health promotion?" Since the question was open-ended without any list of possibilities from which to choose, it was surprising to find such a consensus for the following four factors.

1. High medical costs. No surprise here. The opportunity inherent in adversity seems to be widely believed to be an asset to the growth of the wellness movement.

2. Dissatisfaction with the current state of the health care system. Again, this should not surprise *anyone,* although the adjectives used to express displeasure were interesting to read.

3. Expanded public awareness and interest in self-care and wellness. As of 1985, there were 23 nationally-distributed fitness magazines, according to *Marketing and Media Decisions,* an industry newsletter. Conference participants mentioned the media frequently. Also recognized as influential were books by celebrities. These include Arnold Schwarzenegger, Richard Simmons, and the actresses with diet/exercise books and/or video cassettes, including but surely not limited to Joanie Greggins, Jacki Sorenson, Raquel Welch, Sandahl Bergman, Marie Osmond, Irlene Mandrell, Victoria Principal, Linda Evans, Christie Brinkley and, of course, the Queen of Sweat Jane ("go for the burn") Fonda. For some unknown reason, actors are not as prolific in this field, though someone has "collaborated" with John Travolta on a new fitness book that presumably addresses something the actresses overlooked.

4. The role of business and hospitals. Without all the employee programs, the sense of legitimacy and establishment support would have been absent, and fewer start ups would have occurred.

After these "big four" factors, the consensus fell off, but the list of possibilities did not. All the items noted in the list of ten factors above were repeated in one manner or another. The contenders for the fifth most consequential factor were the impact of one or several mentioned books (e.g., Aerobics); events (Frank Shorter winning the gold at Munich); the proliferation of spas and diet centers/programs; the fact that we are living longer and must contemplate the prospect of life after 65 ("If I had known I would live so long I would have taken better care of myself"); the widespread focus on self responsibility and the growth of "self improvement" programs; the research evidence on the benefits of exercise and other health initiatives; the interest in health insurance reform; the profit potential of wellness for doctors, promoters, medical centers, and entrepreneurs; and the developing evidence for the wellness contention that both the rate and the nature of aging are negotiable.

Many of the suggestions could be placed in several categories, so this list is just suggestive of the richness of contributions. Not so easy to classify but worth thinking about was this contribution from Kurt Unglaub of Ukiah, Ca.: "The fashion industry and the preoccupation with sex, beauty, attractiveness, and the proclivity of society to buy such prescribed images of self. Call it egocentricity."

This commentary is just suggestive of how the wellness movement came about. There is no way to identify all the factors, trends, and events or to set a confident rank order on events. More than anything else, the situation should remind us of the deep cross currents and interconnections between shaping forces in our culture. Some issues transcend specialties. We are more likely to safeguard a commitment to the bigger picture when we recognize this reality.

Knowing something about the background for wellness, we are now in a position to examine how wellness itself, as a movement, came into being and developed to the extent that it has up to 1985.

TWO
The Movement Takes Shape

Development and Growth

The story of wellness, particularly the accounts of pioneering characters, programs, and events, might make a good movie someday, despite the fact that it would probably lack chase scenes, car crashes, blood rituals, homicides, rock music, frontal nudity, and intergalactic battles. For present purposes, however, a short written summary without the sound, fury, and titillation will have to suffice. Use your imagination.

The short history that follows traces the use of the word wellness, not the advance of the major elements which comprise the concept. The distinction is crucial; several volumes would be required to do justice to the individuals and circumstances that figured in the evolution of so inclusive an idea.

To trace but a single wellness dimension, for example, physical fitness, a host of characters would have to be acknowledged who are omitted in this narrower accounting. The history of fitness as a tonic for well being would go back to the Jeffersonian era when we bid adieu to the agrarian society and separated ourselves from a direct link with the food chain. It would require discussion of the influence of the cotton gin and spinning jenny, the automobile, crowding into cities, boredom and monotony, depersonalization, disease, discontent, the division of labor, specialization, and so on. Too often, these forces diminished the individual and brought about deleterious effects on health status. In an earlier time, work and exercise were linked—and this is not a reference to worksite gyms, Nautilus machines, racquetball, or aerobic dance. The advent of tv and automation and other work/exercise savers led to different kinds of customs, and the average state of conditioning—the model of "normalcy," changed. And not for the better in a health sense.

In substantive ways, these forces would later influence the perceived need and climate for the gradual adoption of wellness initiatives.

Therefore, some mention would have to be given to a predecessor group of wellness pioneers if the intent were to trace the evolution of the concept of wellness as opposed to the term. A list of those who helped large numbers of Americans choose loftier, worthier standards of health would be extensive. It would include Thoreau and Emerson, Paul Dudley White, Abraham Maslow, Jesse Owens, Edmund Stieglitz, Paul Bragg, Jack LaLanne, Tom Cureton,

Gayelord Hauser, the Rodales, and many more. Halbert L. Dunn, the modern pioneer of the word wellness that incorporated so many of the principles promoted by these forerunners of the wellness movement, acknowledged these roots in his book *High Level Wellness* and in several articles.

In short, many of our ancestors lived wellness lifestyles without benefit of the phrase. To borrow a line from John Houseman of Smith Barney ad fame, they did it "the old fashioned way—they earned it" by figuring it out for themselves. In so doing, they made it possible for us to build on their sundry methods and ideas.

Oddly, except for the mention of the five individuals noted immediately below (Dr. Halbert L. Dunn and the four "early promoters"), very few respondents had much to offer regarding wellness events and players. Most focused on other questions, and used some variation of the phrase "this is your expertise; I do not have a handle on how wellness itself got underway."

So, with the admission that this interpretation, even more so than the previous material, is almost entirely one person's view, here is a synopsis of wellness, circa mid-fifties to mid-eighties.

Halbert L. Dunn

Anyone writing about the history of wellness would have an easy time at the beginning of the endeavor. Regarding the origin there is no doubt. It began with a retired public health service physician, who in the 1950s began lecturing in the Washington, D.C. area and writing articles about an idea he called "high level wellness." A series of 29 lectures on this topic delivered at a Unitarian Church were printed in 1961. The book was titled *High Level Wellness*.[60] It did not make any best-seller lists, but it did influence a few health professionals, years later, in places distant from the capitol. The book was Dr. Dunn's way of expressing his belief in an interrelated world populated by interdependent humans and creatures ("little beasties"). He stressed the importance of mind/body/spirit connections, the need for personal satisfactions and valued purposes, and a view of health as dramatically more than non-illness.

Four "Early Promoters"

One of the many prominent contemporary wellness advocates who have claimed Dunn as the source of their initial interest in the concept is John Travis. Travis should be considered the second major player in the recent evolution of the wellness movement. Travis got the idea for his pioneering Wellness Resource Center (WRC) from Dr. Dunn's book and articles, and became the first physician to offer wellness services and educational opportunities to the general public and other health professionals. These seminars, along with the development of the WRC and a series of articles by and about Dr. Travis,[61] came into being in 1975 and continued into the early 1980s. During this time, Travis published a *Wellness Workbook*[62] and developed several wellness approaches and models.[63]

My book *High Level Wellness: An Alternative to Doctors, Drugs, and Disease* was published in 1977,[64] shortly after an article about Travis appeared in *Prevention Magazine*.[65] The article was the first national publicity given to the wellness approach (and to John Travis); the book provided a framework (five dimensions) and an ethic that would guide most programs through the present era. Most professionals now active in the wellness movement drew their initial information from this book and related articles and/or from one of the "wellness gypsies" who traveled throughout North America on a wellness lecture circuit. Two of these wellness promoters (Travis and yours truly) have already been mentioned; the others are Robert Allen and William Hettler. A few words about each are in order.

Robert Allen of Morristown, N.J., developed the Lifegain model, the original systematic approach to understanding and selectively changing cultures in order to support wellness intentions. Allen's Lifegain program is in use in thirty-five major medical centers and over 100 corporations; his books and Lifegain materials (slide/tape packages, booklets, and videotapes) are standard resources in the more sophisticated wellness programs.[66]

To appreciate the Lifegain system, consider the following discussion and test taken from the first issue of the *ARDELL WELLNESS REPORT.** This culture awareness type of material is a key part of the wellness movement; my own efforts such as this commentary are very much inspired by Bob Allen's books, lectures and pamphlets.

> Ever wonder why everybody does not live a wellness lifestyle? Probably not, because it's obvious to you.
>
> For reasons of good fortune, fate, divine plan, personal ingenuity, or just by accident, you found yourself reinforced in varied ways to live in a sensible, satisfying way consistent with Nature's laws, human performance discoveries, and assorted principles for what Satchel Paige called "right livin." In short, chances are good that you did not have to be heroic to pull "it" (a wellness lifestyle) off.
>
> The vast majority of people have *not* had the benefit of such reinforcement.
>
> Here's a little test you can use with your friends, relatives, co-workers, and perfect strangers to generate a discussion on the subject of whether or not our environments and associations are making us sick.
>
> To add interest to the test, make up an interpretive scoring system. For example, there are fourteen questions on the following Ardell Culture Test. Suggest to your victims that there is overwhelming scientific evidence that shows, as sure as smoking causes hair on the palms, that you are in big trouble if you answer "Yes, it is normal around here" to *five* or

*For a sample copy of the REPORT, send a SASE (¢.40) to: ARDELL WELLNESS REPORT, c/o PLANNING FOR WELLNESS, 706 RUTH DRIVE, PLEASANT HILL, CA 94523

more of these statements. Then, cross your fingers and tell them that affirmative responses to *eight* or more of the statements represents Undertaker City. You don't want to carry this too far, but if you think your target can handle it and might benefit from a good fright, mention that *ten* or more guarantees everlasting spiritual hangnail and tooth decay. By this point, they should realize that you are full of it but have a considerable interest in taking the test anyway.

Enough introduction. Here is the *Ardell Culture Test*. Good luck.

It's normal around here for people:

To celebrate special occasions with sweets or alcohol or both.

To drink coffee throughout the day because it's so readily available.

To not wear seat belts, to not exercise daily, and to eat junk food.

To ignore the 55 mph speed limit, stop signs, and traffic lights if it looks like you can get away with it.

To tolerate tobacco odors and smoke because smokers have rights too, and you don't want to be pushy or a crank.

To think you're weird if you take time out to close your eyes and relax several times throughout the day to balance or calm yourself.

To take pills or go to a doctor when you are not feeling well, or to pass out aspirins and other medications to each other.

To avoid expressing feelings because that makes you seem strange.

To get positive reinforcement for being rushed, harried, or drawn in appearance—because the more harried you appear, the harder you must be working.

To complain a lot about the job, the boss, the weather, the President, the economy, each other, the food, local teams, and/or parts of your body.

To get feedback only when you have screwed up.

To receive attention when you are down, ill, discouraged, saddened, and otherwise mired in the "Slough of Despond" than when you arrive at work ready to take on the world, jumping up and down with enthusiasm, urging fellow employees to "soar with the eagles" and accomplish great things today, etc.

To tolerate or even ignore the potential harm of advertising during sports programming that promotes youthful drinking (e.g., the use by Miller and Budweiser of athletic heroes depicted in bars having exuberant good times guzzling the sponsors products).

To not give priority to quality of life issues, such as protecting the environment, having fun in life, enjoying and taking in work, experiencing spiritual growth, and reaching out to others.

Now that you have their attention and they want to know what the test *really* indicates, smile and explain how it just exemplifies how so many things we take for granted are truly inimical even to our best efforts to live healthy lifestyles. Note also that a conscious recognition of these factors and an appreciation of the power of the cultures we seldom think about is an important first part in organizing to improve our environments. Finally, try to conclude before you become a nuisance. Perhaps you can say something witty and/or profound to the effect that they can promote their chances of sustaining healthier lifestyles by redesigning such habits and customs as those noted in the test, in concert with others over time. Then get out of there before you wear out your welcome.

William Hettler, Director of the Student Health Service at the University of Wisconsin, Stevens Point, was the first to apply wellness in a University setting. Unlike Travis, Allen, and yours truly, Hettler managed to integrate wellness into his full-time responsibilities and also travel around the country presenting lectures on wellness techniques and principles. His work at the University of Wisconsin, Stevens Point resulted in an innovative, student-led wellness model that has been adopted in some form by hundreds of colleges and universities. In addition, Hettler's efforts led to the annual wellness conferences at Stevens Point which have probably done more than anything else to fuel the movement and enable its gradual spread to all regions of the United States.

In the early days of the wellness movement, the four early promoters were something akin to being "rock stars" of that period. Their ideas seemed a bit outrageous, they were in demand everywhere, and they rather "stood out." No longer. Today, every town and borough has several individuals, as often as not physicians turned health promoters, who can and do give outstanding lectures and seminars on wellness. The "old timers" are still alive, thank goodness, not entirely forgotten (certainly not by loyal family members), but the need for their globe-trotting predilections has been moderated. This, of course, reflects the maturing and spread of the movement. (Let's hope for my sake that it does not get out of hand—be aware that I'm still available for lectures, seminars, and elegant sea cruises!)

National Wellness Conferences

When America was having its bi-centennial birthday party in the summer of 1976, another institution was being founded in the Nation's heartland. This was the Wisconsin wellness festival, known then as the Wellness Promotion Strategies Conference. Less than fifty people attended and the event was directed to and led by local interests. But the conference was a success for the participants and the sponsoring University, and the idea of a week-long annual gathering was born. The need for a gathering of this kind was apparent in the years to follow, as each succeeding conference drew larger and more enthusiastic followers from increasing distant places. As of the 1985 edition held from July 21st through the 27th, approximately 7,000 persons have participated in the Stevens Point festivals. No other event has enabled as much wellness education, has provided as much encouragement and support for enthusiasts, or engendered as many spin-off seminars/articles/and programs as these national conferences.

Credit for the success of the festival belongs to many organizers, volunteers, speakers, participants, student assistants, and unsung others (such as the food service people and the entertainers). However, three movers and shakers from the University have shared a triumvirate approach as co-directors of the conference since 1976: Bill Hettler, Fred Leafgren, and Denny Elsenrath. This team has earned special mention.

In recent years, the Institute for Lifestyle Improvement has evolved into an organization which provides wellness services to public and private agencies, conducts research on lifestyle improvement activities, and provides continuing education seminars. It is the sponsor of the annual festival, now simply called the National Wellness Conference. The Institute sells a popular lifestyle assessment questionnaire and a variety of audiovisual and print materials, including a Fit Stop portable assessment tool and a set of self care modules. They have come a long way since 1976, but then so has the wellness movement.

It will be interesting to see what the Institute is selling ten years from now; it will be even more interesting to observe and perhaps attend the 25th National Wellness Conference in the Year 2000. (But let's not rush things.) For a brochure about the next National Wellness Conference or other products and services noted above, write to Jane Jones, Ph.D., Assistant Director, Institute For Lifestyle Improvement, Delzell Hall, University of Wisconsin–Stevens Point, Stevens Point, Wi. 54481 or call (715) 346–2611.

In addition to the works of Halbert L. Dunn, the four early promoters, and the Stevens Point Wellness Conferences, seven other events stand out as influential during the early years.

Frost Valley YMCA

One of these is the programming for young people at the Frost Valley YMCA.[67] Under the leadership of Halbe Brown and Michael Ketchum and backed by the Victoria Foundation, political leaders in Newark, N.J., all the early promoters noted above, and many others, this YMCA made wellness the priority concept for its 3000 plus camper population beginning in the summer of 1978. Over the years, the leadership developed innovative ways to integrate wellness into camp life, and received a good deal of public attention in doing so.[68] By the early 1980s, Frost Valley's wellness promoters found themselves assisting other YMCA managers to design and carry out similar efforts on a national basis. At the present time, a full-scale consultation service is provided, and materials are sent regularly to youth groups on request explaining how, when, and why to initiate wellness into YMCA programming.

Health Systems Agencies (HSA'S)

Not so well known, even among the wellness cogniscenti, is the potent role once played by regional Health Systems Agencies (HSA's). These organizations, some of which still exist, were largely supported by federal funds but directed by local boards of area residents with interests in health care issues. Their role, like the comprehensive health planning groups they superseded, was to recommend ways to make the medical system more effective, efficient, and equitable. Without authority to do much more than to delay and frustrate hospital construction and other capital projects, their public visibility and community status were marginal. Yet, a quiet effort was made by a number of planning agency directors and staff members from 1976 to 1979 to steer the HSA's toward an advocacy position of wellness promotion.[69] Remarkably, this effort was succeeding, in part because the usual and customary "omnibus tinkering" role assigned to HSA's was stultifying for all involved citizen volunteer and professional staff members alike; and in part because area planning for desired future states was a logical and attractive forum for the discussion and integration of wellness goals and objectives. For these reasons and a few harder to trace motivations, a full third of the HSA's then in existence were advocating wellness. Wellness was seen as a blueprint for a future health system wherein genuine advances in health status as well as cost constraints on medical spending could be realized.[70]

Unfortunately, the advance of wellness issues, an activity of great interest and "sex appeal," led to a neglect of the drudgery of cost containment duties (e.g., certificate of need hearings). The Federal funding agencies, not yet sympathetic or informed about the nature and promise of the wellness movement, stepped in and brought a halt to these "unauthorized," non-priority endeavors.[71] But the good had been done and a lot more awareness of the ideas associated with the movement had spread even further throughout the medical and corporate establishments.

American Hospital Association

The next significant advance occurred when the American Hospital Association established a Center for Health Promotion, and directed the small staff assigned to it to assist member hospitals in developing health promotion/ wellness programming. The Center did very well, disseminating newsletters and reports, providing consultations, conducting conference calls and, most significantly, sponsoring conferences to encourage the development of hospital-based wellness centers.[72] In effect, these meetings, held at least twice yearly and sometimes more often, provided the same professional group network for hospital wellness promoters that the University of Wisconsin–Stevens Point festivals provided everyone else.

Swedish Medical Center

The Swedish Medical Center in Englewood (Denver), Colorado, deserves a special place if there is ever built a "Wellness Hall of Fame." It was the first hospital to establish a wellness center and to hire a full-time staff to provide wellness classes and activities for employees and community residents. More important than being first, the Swedish effort was a success financially, politically (within the medical center), and programmatically. Soon after its founding in 1978, the Center was providing training seminars and materials to *other hospitals* as well as interested businesses, doctor groups, clinics, and schools in the Denver area. At the present time, it has nearly twenty major wellness service contracts with institutional clients throughout the country.[73]

Governors' Councils

Another positive influence, starting around 1980, was the creation of State Governors' Councils on Wellness (and Physical Fitness, Health Promotion, etc.). Twenty-two of these councils, usually funded in part by state legislatures and appointed by the chief executive of each state, are in existence at the present time. The first and most notable, by far, is the Wisconsin Council. This initiative was of special consequence because of the fact that it had a million dollars to play with, more accurately to use, as wellness "seed" money for promoting local innovations. While only a small number of awards were granted due to limited funds, nearly all the two hundred organizations which prepared fund requests went ahead without the Council's help. This seems to reflect some manner of testimony to the inherent energy and enthusiasm associated with planning health-enhancing endeavors. This is particularly so when such activities are conducted along lines that reinforce personal responsibility, recognize near-term results, and encourage individualized approaches for changing norms and sustaining good behavioral intentions.

Industry Models: Sentry and Scherer

The support for wellness by certain corporate interests must also be recognized. Most of the programs noted in the previous section as predisposing, "pave-the-way" for wellness were (and remain) risk-reduction/health promotion oriented. Only a few have the qualities defined in the beginning of this article as unique to wellness. Two of the industry initiatives certainly warrant special mention in this respect: Sentry Insurance (Stevens Point, Wisconsin) and Scherer Lumber (Minneapolis, Minnesota). The models used in both cases are of interest to other companies evaluating the returns from such non-traditional human resource investments; for this reason, the successes of both will have effects beyond the benefits derived by the affected employees.

Other Crucial Factors

Finally, there is a vast "other" category much larger than those noted above. It includes all the individual physicians, nurses, and administrators who encouraged and worked for wellness initiatives in thousands of ways and places too numerous to mention here (or even to know about). It includes other early promoters, especially Richard Schafer (designed, taught, and secured approval for the first required high school wellness course) in Madison, Wisconsin, and Leland Kaiser at the University of Colorado, Denver (one of the most popular lecturers on wellness in the beginning period). It includes scores of public and private associations that supported the growth of the wellness movement by scheduling keynote addresses and workshops on the topic at their annual meetings. In short, it would include a great many players and events not known to this chronicler but which no doubt functioned in all manner of crucial ways to provide wellness with the prospects that it enjoys today.

A current marketing strategy that is proving quite successful for medical centers is to sponsor "executive retreats." These three and four day intensive seminars provide corporate leaders with a personal exposure to the nature and value of wellness programming—and usually lead to follow-up engagements between the sponsoring medical center and the employer whose chief executive has become an advocate for the value of health promotion for others at his or her worksite. This approach has been used for years by St. Luke's in Kansas City, St. Vincent's in Indianapolis, and The Mason Clinic in Seattle—and the results have been spectacular. Eve Stern, Director of Corporate Accounts at The Mason Clinic, wrote that "we have derived so much business from the last Retreat (at the Rosario Retreat Center on Orcas Island) that we are considering waiting a year before doing another."

There is another factor at work in the growth of the wellness movement, one more influential to the movement if less consequential to the public weal than all the above mentioned characters and events. It is the growth of the wellness job market. This is the mystery factor. However profound, necessary, and attractive a concept wellness might be, it would have few effective promoters if there were a scarcity of opportunities to earn at least a modest living from such pursuits.

The first persons to succeed (in a fashion) in supporting themselves in the full-time business of wellness promotion were John Travis and this writer, beginning around 1975. John did it through a combination of wellness center program offerings, seminars and products; my own method was a combination of books, lectures, and consultations. The advent of hospital based and corporate wellness programming in 1978 ushered in the period of part-time, and later full-time opportunities. At this point and not before could it be said that the wellness movement stood a reasonable prospect of growth and continuance.

At the present time (1985), the number of individuals generating income from wellness endeavors on either a full or at least half time basis has grown to 2,479, and is expected to skyrocket to 5028 by the end of 1986.*

Naturally, a drop in public interest in wellness lectures, video tapes, seminars, and programs would result in a rapid decline in the number of practitioners, promoters, and activists in and outside the health field; a rise in interest, on the other side, would have just the opposite effect. Fortunately, the latter seems the likelier prospect, in part because of the growing corporate initiatives and in part because to think otherwise is depressing. At this point, it might be useful to consider the nature of these prospects in light of the "megatrends" forecast for the years to come.

*You may be wondering where I got these figures. The answer, of course, is that I made them up. Artistic license, you might call it.

THREE
The Future Lies Ahead

Trends Affecting the Wellness Movement

Predictions are always hazardous, especially those pertaining to the future.[74] Nevertheless, enough is known from the writings of futurists to anticipate major developments and to speculate on consequences of these developments for the growth (or decline) of wellness.

What trends, therefore, seem to be of most consequence? The survey of "experts" provided remarkable consistency in identifying the most salient likely directions. A summary should be of interest.

1. Government expenditures on health are projected to exceed 4% of the GNP by 1985.[75]
    a. The health care industry will take more responsibility for educating consumers on how and why to initiate behavior change.
    b. Political pressures for wellness and health promotion at the federal and state level will increase as the allocation of health resources are decided at these governmental levels.
    c. Issues of equity of access to wellness services will become more acute—look for unions to introduce wellness into the collective bargaining process.
    d. There will be increased government regulations requiring health promotion and wellness endeavors as a means of controlling costs.
    e. Care will be rationed by the government, which will also fix a minimum ratio of health promotion to health care services.
    f. Business will take a more active role in the shaping of health promotion program methods and defining the range of costs for such endeavors.
2. There will be more than a 40% increase in the number of practicing physicians during the 1980s.
    a. Physician income will decline.
    b. There will be changes in medical education with more focus on lifestyle and environmental influences on health and disease states.

33

c. There will be improved access to health care as physicians are forced into underserved areas and under represented specialties.
d. There will be less specialization and a great deal more focus on the whole individual.
e. Physicians will work as salaried employees of hospitals and health promotion groups.
f. A recent decline in the sale of tranquilizers and other medications suggest a reduced future reliance on drugs.
g. Physicians will do new health promotion tasks not now associated with the physician role.
h. Physicians will become the most effective professional force in advocating wellness lifestyles, inasmuch as they will be seeing the sick people who need training for wellness more than the basically healthy who currently use these services and centers the most.

3. Rapid technological development will continue to shape the practice of medicine.
   a. Premature use of inadequately tested new technologies that have profit value could have harmful effects, thereby counterbalancing rises in health status.
   b. The media fascination with dramatic medical practices might make people more complacent about individual responsibility for self-care.

4. Developments in wellness and health promotion represent a shift of power and responsibility from the professional health care system to the individual.
   a. We can look for a trend away from high-tech, institutionally-based treatment in tertiary medical centers to increasing reliance on home remedies and personalized self-health initiatives consistent with maximum personal autonomy. Naisbitt has popularized the phrase "from high tech to high touch" to capture this ideal. In his words: "The focus of health care is shifting from the short-term treatment of illness to the long-term attainment of wellness. Regarded by some as a fad, wellness is a trend that is here to stay. Are hospitals in the wellness or sickness business? Over the long term, our prediction is that hospitals will have to reconceptualize their business to fit with the wellness trend."[76]
   b. Alternative delivery systems and new contract approaches between employees and institutional providers will proliferate. Wellness may be built into many of these contracts.
   c. Employers will become more aggressive and creative in their efforts to reduce health care costs.

d. Insurance benefits will be evaluated with respect to paybacks for nonutilization or reduced utilization. Expect incentives for wellness and support for improved versions of the Blue Shield "Stay Well" Plan.

e. The emphasis on health promotion programs in the workplace will lessen dependence on medical care.

f. There will be more aggressive bargaining for group health promotion benefits at reduced rates.

g. The public will be given a double message: one about medical wonders; the other about the benefits of personal responsibility to lessen one's need for such wonders.

The debate will heat up regarding ethical issues related to new medical technologies that enable life and (time of) death decisions not previously thinkable.

Item "c" above pertaining to workplace health promotion warrants special attention. American corporations have a major role to play, both as market areas for wellness programming by institutional vendors (i.e., hospitals) and as the vital opportunity site for employees who choose wellness over mediocrity. A brief sampling of wellness activities at the workplace is in order.

*Quaker Oats has a three-part program that is designed to encourage employees to use medical care judiciously, to shop wisely for medical vendors, and to promote wellness. The company uses a medical reimbursement plan that gives each worker a "health expense account" up to $300. annually. Unused portions at year's end are given to employees in cash.

*FMC Corporation, a $3.5 billion producer of machinery and chemicals, offers its 31,000 employees (at 100 plants and mines) wellness programs in the belief that "healthier employees will cost less in terms of absenteeism, disability, and medical expenses . . . and because we really care about our employees." (American Medical News, August 17, 1984, p. 1.) Yet, this program and others like it are widely perceived as a corporate "leap of faith" or, as Thomas J. Peters, co-author of the book *In Search of Excellence* put it— part of the "emerging new wave of humanism at the workplace."

A major goal of current business wellness programs is simply to make workers more conscious of positive health. At Xerox Corporation, C. Craig Wright, M.D. discussed culture change as the program goal. A major part of this change, he said, is just to communicate to each employee that "the individual is responsible for his or her health."

Another popular wellness goal is better employee relations. At Tenneco, programs are designed to increase satisfaction with the company. A corporate Vice-President, Dr. Edward Bernacki, said wellness is "an employee benefit that helps the company recruit and retain productive workers." Tenneco has reported a strong correlation between participation in the programs and job performance—a correlation that could do much to stimulate the wellness movement.

Another trend affecting the spread of wellness at the worksite is the entry of "big time" entrepreneurs into the wellness market. People's Drug Stores, for example, has started a "Feeling Fine" division to promote wellness to business—and already lists the U.S. Senate and the Mid-Atlantic Coca-Cola Bottling Co. as clients. The President of the operation, David Forman, offered the following observation:

> Wellness is in its infancy. There's a growing realization that wellness programs are the key to containing health care costs.

A final note on the workplace concerns productivity. There are some wellness promoters, David W. Randle and Robert Allen among them, who see productivity gains as the most exciting development affecting the future of wellness. The following statement by Dr. Randle explains the theory behind this latest application of wellness. The overall goal is to support and encourage more effective organizations by fostering healthier employees in the context of healthier communities.

Clearly, the future is no longer what it used to be.

> The Breakthrough Performance Program provides individuals, organizations, and communities the knowledge, skills, and support to live life more enjoyably as well as productively.
>
> The program seeks to create lifestyles where people are more often in harmony with themselves, with others, and with their environment. This is accomplished by both breaking through self-imposed limitations and creating and fostering healthy cultural norms.
>
> The Breakthrough Performance Program draws not only from the large body of wellness literature (i.e., Ardell, Allen, Travis, etc.) but also from the normative systems approach for individual and cultural change, techniques for training world class athletes, lessons learned from breakthrough organizations, transpersonal psychology, metaphors from the natural environment, the martial arts of Tai Chi Chuan and Aikido, and many other processes and techniques.
>
> Some of the program components include computerized individual and organizational analysis, breakthrough performance training workshops, program modules in such areas as nutrition and weight control, physical fitness, stress management, personal care and prevention of illness and injury, personal growth and self-realization, and the core of all the dimensions—one's own spiritual orientation and ethics.

The following test, which appeared in the second issue of the WELLNESS REPORT, is intended to approximate the extent to which your work environment supports and encourages you to be a "breakthrough performer." Another benefit of the test is consciousness-raising: if these conditions seem foreign to the reality of your day-to-day work life, it may be time to join with others to change aspects of the norms which block your best efforts. Failing that, it may be time to update your resume.

A Breakthrough Performance Test

On a scale of one to five, how well is your organization doing in:

Change and Innovation

*People feel free to take risks and experiment in their work. _____

*Creativity is affirmed daily. _____

*A few key advisors take the responsibility for projects as opposed to the assignment of projects to committees. _____

Motivation

*People feel that they make a powerful difference and are involved in experiences that prove it. _____

*Salaries meet basic needs and also provide incentives. _____

*People are rewarded and recognized for excellent performance. _____

Conflict Resolution

*Conflicts are resolved with win/win solutions or are mediated by nonaffected third parties. _____

*People constructively confront negative behavior when it occurs. _____

*People avoid blame placing and finger pointing as a method of problem solving. _____

Participative Management

*The decision making process is highly participatory. _____

*People emphasize cooperation over competition among members of the organization. _____

*People help set their own work objectives and work methods. _____

Communication

*Peoples beliefs are congruent with their actions. _____

*People understand how their work relates to the goals or values of the organization. _____

*People actively seek out the ideas and opinions of others. _____

Leadership

*Leaders follow up on problems and new ideas in a swift way. _____

*Leaders show a balanced concern between the quality work that has to be done and the people who are doing it. _____

*Leaders are actively involved in the provision of quality service and they model the behavior they expect of others. _____

Team Building

*Some meetings focus on nothing but individual and/or group achievements. _____

*Support for and caring of associates is strongly emphasized. _____

*People are concerned about the success of the work group. _____

Stress Management

*The work environment is relaxing and families are included in some of the organization's programs. _____

*Fitness facilities and programs are available and their use is encouraged. _____

*The organization provides the necessary staff, programs, or other resources to assist people under stress or having personal problems. _____

Follow Through/Results Orientation

*Change efforts focus on measurable results. _____

*Quality is something upper management not only talks about but also does something about. _____

*Management acts quickly and decisively on quality improvement suggestions. _____

Interpretation

There are nine performance categories. The highest possible score is 45; the lowest is 9. If you gave your organization 36 or more points, you are either self employed and doing well or working for a company that knows how to support excellence in its employees. If you gave it between 27 and 35 points, it has excellent possibilities. Work with it. If, however, it got less than 27 performance points from you, take heed. As Plato observed: you are in jeopardy if you must be a hero or a fool to do what is right.

Bill Hettler has an interesting suggestion for his physician brethren whom he urges to support and endorse wellness programming:

> It's going to happen anyway so why not get in front and pretend you are leading?

38

Three other trends, beyond the health care or medical system, seem of note. One concerns the aging of the U.S. population. It is widely expected that, barring a nuclear or other disaster of unparalleled magnitude, the number of citizens in this country over age 65 will expand to 17 percent of the population by the year 2030.[77] This contrasts with 11 percent today. This means, according to a Census Bureau report entitled "America In Transition: An Aging Society," that one in every five Americans will be 65 or older in less than half a century and that the number of elderly will double by 2020. The raw numbers paint a clearer picture of the situation: instead of 25.5 million (1980) over age 65, there will be 64.3 million mature folks by 2030. If you take care of yourself, you may be one of them.

While few readers of this book are likely to need more reasons to take good care of themselves, this first trend of an aging population has a couple interesting implications. One involves the impact of an older population of retirees on the cost to business of payments for health insurance. While this is not as yet a well-publicized problem, there is a potential crisis ahead for U.S. business in the funding and liability of health care retirement plans.

A recent issue of Business Week ("Health Plans May Leave Retirees Out in the Cold," December 17, 1984, pp. 105–6) revealed that 98 percent of U.S. companies are failing to back up their promises to retirees to continue health insurance through the retirement years with any kind of funding scheme guarantees. As a result, health insurance payments for retirees has become a growing deferred obligation that is increasingly hard to meet with current revenues. Southern New England Telephone is sometimes cited as illustrative of the problem. Six years ago, the company had 2,825 retired workers and the cost of their health insurance was $1.47 million. Last year, the number of retirees to be covered had grown to 3,986 and the cost was $6.33 million. As with most businesses, these funds have to come from current income, unlike pension funding which is paid for well in advance of employee retirement. It is estimated that the Nation's 500 major industrial companies have an unfunded liability for medical protection in excess of $2 trillion; the liability of all businesses is said to be incalculable. And the problem will get worse as health care costs continue to rise faster than the rate of inflation, retirees remain eligible for benefits for a longer period due to increased life expectancy, and the trend toward early retirements continues—further raising the liability of corporations.

A wellness interpretation of this situation is to adopt a do-it-yourself posture of self reliance while taking whatever political action seems feasible to force companies to put funds aside for retirement health plans (in concert with organized retirement groups). Under this do-it-yourself posture, your attitude toward the prospects of employer-paid health insurance might be expressed as follows: Forget it—or at least do not count on medical insurance payments coming from the company you worked for all your life. You probably are not planning to retire on your social security payments, either. Think of a commitment to wellness as a form of lifestyle Keough or I.R.A. program—and do everything you can now to improve the chances that you will not need help from your employer or the government later.

Another implication of the first mentioned trend of an aging America is that we could see a major change in the culture of older people—changes that invite more vigorous lifestyles and a rejection of the rocking-chair images of the past. With new images will come different expectations, norms, values, and attitudes of older citizens—and support for wellness programming. If this occurs, then active seniors will comprise a new wellness marketing area. Sheldon Goldberg, head of the American Association of Homes for the Aging, referred to contemporary nursing homes for compliant patient/residents as "the iron lung of geriatrics." He expects that the coming generation of residents will be more self-sufficient, demanding of involvement in health care and other issues affecting them, active in their own scheduling, and highly responsive to health promotion and wellness programming. The implication, loud and clear, of this trend is that seniors are and will remain a major opportunity and responsibility for those involved in community wellness.

A second basic trend is that consumers are taking much more interest in and responsibility for their own health. This trend has been building for at least a decade. It is getting stronger. The editor of Medical Self Care forecasts a $24 billion annual savings by 1985 as Americans learn to practice simple self-care remedies and thereby avoid unnecessary but costly encounters with medical professionals.[78] Educational software for home computers had sales of $70 million last year; industry leaders expect this to go to $1 billion by 1987. At least $100 million of this will be in self-care software. Another research firm (Creative Strategies International) estimates that consumers will be spending $10 billion a year on medical self-care equipment by 1990.[79]

Another dramatic indication of consumer interest in health is seen in the booming market for exercise equipment. In 1984, total sales topped the one billion dollar mark—double that of 1981. (Source: USA Today, October 16, 1984, p. 38.)

Consider the opportunities this presents for wellness educators—for some as authors and/or distributors of these materials, for others as users and promoters of that which works best.

The last trend to mention, though there are doubtless many others which will affect the future of wellness, is in the area of health education for children. The emphasis will increasingly be placed on young age cohorts, particularly the 8 to 12 year old set, as primary targets for good health habit training. These efforts will not take the form of didactic lectures and pamphlets about diseases, infirmities, and other negative consequences of smoking, alcohol abuse, drug use, and the like. The new programming, as foreshadowed by the Frost Valley YMCA experience, is more likely to be integrated with values training, self-esteem building, and varied fun situations. Wellness lifestyle practices and knowledge skills will be integrated into the routine of the learning environment—such an ethic will pervade the classroom atmosphere. It will not be necessary to be exceptional to learn about, practice, and adopt health-enhancing ways of functioning in the new educational circumstances.

Yet, the optimism concerning future trends and their promising implications for wellness should be tempered with a willingness to face the challenges that could untrack our young, undeveloped movement. A look at some of these concerns is in order.

FOUR
The Challenges We Face

Counter-Trends and Hazards

The preceding trends might leave a reader with a sense of excitement and anticipation, which is certainly better than being bored and depressed if you believe in a wellness approach to life. Yet, rose-colored glasses should not be worn for long periods without occasional reality checks. There are a few disquieting counter-trends or hazards that all involved in the wellness business need to be aware of. In many cases, even more is required: something constructive should be done about them.

The major challenge, as already mentioned, is the need to make wellness information available and attractive to less advantaged population groups. The value of wellness for poor people who are undereducated and oftentimes far less healthy than their potentials would allow is unquestioned. They often need and want assistance in developing healthy life habits and overcoming negative addictions, such as smoking, alcohol and drug abuse, poor eating habits and lack of significant exercise. Like middle class folks, they would love to experience a higher sense of self-respect and self-esteem, learn to manage stress in their daily lives, and find work and avocations that add meaning and dignity to their existence. These are not desires and qualities unique to a privileged minority. They are part of the agenda for all who share the human condition.

It is just their misfortune that they often have so many other concerns to deal with first such as finding (and maintaining) decent housing, feeding themselves and their families, and so on. Helping all Americans to deal with these overarching problems *is a wellness issue!*

Wellness promoters have not faced up to it as yet, in part because there is so little as individuals they can do about it once they "face up to it," but all our nation's social/economic failings are wellness issues. This means that wellness is a political process, a basic part of the larger agenda of public policy deliberations affecting the way resources are allocated and rights preserved.

A second challenge, related to the first, is to develop new ways to present the case for health-enriching values and behaviors that are entertaining, substantive, accessible, and appealing to those who need wellness the most. Too much current energies are spent (especially by lecturers like this writer) "preaching to the choir" of true believers: the no nukes, save-the-whale vegetarian triathles who meditate, take food supplements, and eat tofu. How do we "sell" wellness to the folks who crowd the sports stadia, the bars, bowling alleys, and fast food emporiums? How do we "win friends and influence people" for wellness who watch daily soap operas, crowd the bingo parlors, and play video games? There are no easy answers to this challenge, but it makes sense to start thinking in such terms.

These are the biggies. There are other challenges, not simple and easy to confront but manageable by comparison. They include:

1. Reaching the healthy young. A lot of attention is showered on problem kids in our school system. That is OK, but the vast majority of "normal" youngsters are allowed, through neglect, to develop poor lifestyle habits highly injurious to their best possible futures. This young age cohort, pre-high school, might be the highest payoff group for concerted, long term public wellness investments.

2. Less cost containment, more health enhancement. Our government is pulling out nearly all stops to control the high costs of the medical care system. The current Administration is proposing or has achieved new taxes on health insurance benefits, price fixing on 468 Medicare diagnoses, raised charges to Medicare patients, and so on. The private sector is pushing surgi-centers, corporate coalitions for better rates, competition between vendors, and so on. Unfortunately, the Administration is completely overlooking a different approach: helping people stay well in the first place. A few positive incentives (e.g., food stamp bonuses, tax credits) for wellness initiatives might prove a great deal more cost effective than simply denying or restricting medical benefit payments after the fact.

Perhaps the Administration should institute a 469th diagnosis related group (DRG) for which the government will reimburse medical providers and institutions. This DRG number 469 would be for incipient worseness—and would enable a medical institution to admit individuals (on an outpatient basis) for some form of wellness training before they qualify for one of the other 468 DRG categories! This DRG would, of course, be the least expensive of all the DRG categories: a very modest sum, say, $100 per person per year, should suffice for counseling and training patients who smoke, are sedentary, bored, or just stressed out, a little depressed, mired in low self esteem, or who otherwise seem to be excellent candidates for a lifestyle refresher and "picker-upper."

3. Going beyond the media hype. A lot of people have an unrealistic picture of physical well-being and conditioning in America. People *appear* to be running, lifting, aerobic dancing, and otherwise working off excess fat, building strong hearts and clear, HDL-type arteries.

But, look closer: as noted above, not all social classes are doing it. Recent findings from the President's Council on Fitness and Sports tell another side of the story. The so-called "fitness boom" is dismissed "as a media mirage that has had little impact on society as a whole." As the following indicates, the only "boom" out there is an equipment boom. People buy a lot of fitness stuff (especially running shoes) because it's fashionable or trendy, not always for the purposes for which it was intended.

Half of the country's 160 million adults never engage in vigorous physical activity. One-third of all American children are overweight, and more than half of all children cannot meet average fitness standards for their age group. The physical fitness of American boys and girls has not significantly improved in the last 17 years. School districts across the country are lowering physical education requirements in response to budget cuts. Few of the elderly, the poor and the less-educated realize that proper exercise can greatly improve their health and the overall quality of their lives.[80]

A recent survey by the American Sports Data Research Group adds credibility to this perspective. They found that people who consider themselves either joggers or runners had rather unambitious views concerning the requirements for joining such a category. Only 3.6 percent of the "joggers" ran more than 40 miles per week and 68 percent ran *less than* 10 miles per week. Overall, 29 percent of adults own running shoes but less than 12 percent actually run! One conclusion from all this was that an army of "non-participant trendy types wear the uniform but rarely run, even for a bus. They buy the paraphernalia instead to symbolize identification with the ideal of fitness, yet for varied reasons have not genuinely become part of it."

Another interpretation is that survey-takers need to tighten up their standards of what constitutes fitness activities worth getting excited about. For example, an article in *Medical World News* ("The Fitness Boom," July 23, 1984, pp. 44–56) quoted a sporting goods dealers survey estimating that over 101 million Americans were participating in swimming. Sounds encouraging, doesn't it? Unfortunately, the numbers included an unspecified percentage of "sunbathers and other less active enthusiasts." If memory serves, Dr. Kenneth Cooper awards somewhat fewer points for sunbathing than for lap swimming. In other words, it would be helpful to know how many swim how often for how long if not at what level of intensity; it is in no way helpful to know how many like to sunbathe—unless you are a skin cancer specialist.

4. Downplaying the guilt factor. There is a tendency in most of us to get "uppity" at times about our virtuous ways or at least our good intentions. Our culture is filled with "shoulds." Wellness proponents could easily get caught up in such tendencies, believing as we do

that others *should* also be fit, *should* take responsibility, and so on. No wonder people feel "should upon" at times.

The list of challenges and concerns could go on. There are, for final examples, the following potential hazards with which all wellness promoters must contend:

- Misuse of the word by others (e.g., "colonic wellness"), with attendant credibility setbacks.
- Poor program designs—same effect.
- Cooptation by big business—can you imagine "The Virginia Slims Wellness Festival?"; or "The Budweiser Health Promotion Strategies Conference?".
- The usual, everyday threatened setbacks with which we all must deal (an alarming rise in the number of loonies on the streets, herpes, pot holes, transvestites, nude muggings, soggy rice krispies, and anxieties about toxic wastes, economic collapse, earthquakes, nuclear missiles, and moral absolutists).
- Adoption by a cult. How would business leaders, conservative physicians, and others sensitive to appearances and associations react if wellness were embraced by, let's say, Bhagwan Shree Rajneesh? Or, what if a charismatic cult figure convinced his followers to "get into the cosmic flow" of wellness by wearing orange robes and handing out orange slices on busy street corners. Would wellness as a concept survive such friendly endorsements?

Wellness Conference Participant Opinions

Participants at the wellness conferences who responded to the survey identified many of these factors, and added quite a few others. The specific question that elicited the greatest response was: "What are the current issues, trends, challenges, or hazards which will or could hinder wellness and health promotion in the years to come?"

In descending order of frequency of mention, here is a summary of the responses.

1. Economic barriers to change. This was expressed in varied ways by about a hundred commentators. If wellness programs are largely tailored to the affluent sectors, as is currently the case for all the reasons previously noted, the programming that results will hold little appeal for the "under-classes." In addition, whether appealing or not, poor people will simply not be able to afford to pay for such options as classes, courses, training programs and the like.

46

A representative statement expressive of this concern is as follows:

The upward trend of inflation could lock out the very people we want to attract to our programming. There must be subsidies from both the public and private sectors to guard against this.

2. Wellness quackery. It was fun reading some of the examples of this "hinder" factor. As a safeguard against lawsuits, no names of quacks will be mentioned. (If you are a quack know that some folks are on to you.) Also in this category would be the "hinder factors" referring to modalities considered bizarre, offensive, and esoteric. However, it would be prudent to remind ourselves that some mighty creative ideas now held as gospel were at one time scorned. Still, this concern is prevalent, as expressed in the following two participant statements:

The adulteration of sound physiology with speculative philosophy (physic phenomena, eastern philosophy, astrology, and so on) serves to discredit wellness and could prove to be its ultimate demise. There is a mind/body connection, but we do not need off-the-wall theories to explain it.

I am concerned that there will be a lot more association of wellness with minority viewpoints of a religious or politically extreme and exclusionary nature, leading to a reaction against the attendant narrowness of its base. This will work to the detriment of sound and sensible efforts.

The real danger will come from the appearance of wellness promoters and other adherents who are *so* radical and preachy as to make the concept a 'holier-than-thou' proposition.

3. The escalation of today's many small wars into a very big war, that is, a nuclear Armageddon that will make any mention of wellness for survivors (assuming there are any) a form of gallows humor.

It was more than a little scary to observe how many people in the forefront of the wellness effort are concerned about this disastrous possibility.

4. The current level of investment in the trappings of the sickness model. There were frequent concerns about the huge investments in pharmaceuticals, high tech equipment, and the training of so many super-specialists. "What will all these people do if there *is* a wellness renaissance?", asked one respondent. "Resist change," was a frequently proffered suggestion.

5. Lack of reimbursement mechanisms. The opportunities range from few to none for most people to choose health-enhancing activities that are reimbursable under Medicare or other government entitlement programs. Unfortunately, the situation is not much better in the private sector.

6. Doctor and other medical sector resistance or non-involvement. The image of doctors as resistant to change in the current system is very

strongly held by the general public, and the individuals closest to the wellness movement hold pictures that are not very different, if the survey respondents truly reflect the perceptions of health activists.

7. A new cure for one or more of the major diseases. This would lessen the appeal of leading healthier lifestyles for some. However, none who suggested this hindering factor seemed to think that such a cure was on the horizon. (There were no suggestions that the Jarvik heart—with its eleven pound portable power system, unproven procedures, and nearly incalculable (certainly unaffordable) costs, is worthy of consideration as a "cure" for heart disease.

8. The persistence of poor methodologies for measuring the effect of our efforts, and in particular for being able to approximate how much health an investor (e.g., an employer) might get back for each dollar invested in (employee) health promotion.

It is important to recognize that the tendency of some health promotion skeptics to wait for further evidence, to conduct more research, or to want to test-market one more process can be a terminal form of paralysis. We have enough evidence already to support the self-evident assertion that individuals with conditioned hearts, slim bodies, positive health habits, high self esteem, and so on live longer and get sick less often than their brothers and sisters whose hearts and stomachs are laden with blubber, who smoke and abuse alcohol, and who bear grudges against themselves and others. There are always those who want to do further research on one thing or another but, after a certain point, you reach diminishing returns from doing so. As Lee Iacocca notes in his best-selling autobiography: "Sometimes you just have to take a chance—and correct your mistakes as you go along." (*Iacocca: An Autobiography,* Bantam Books, Inc., NY, 1984.)

9. Resistance to change. It does not matter how good an idea wellness is: there will remain entrenched tendencies in all of us to resist changes in the status quo.

10. The hazards of governmental intervention. Most of us want to see the government do more, but a lot of people in attenance at the wellness conferences think that such intervention could lead to as much harm as good. The distrust of bureaucracy and the heavy hand of regulators received frequent mention.

11. The diversionary hazard of wellness. What if the wellness revolution leads us to overlook or at least to put less energy into the need for some foundation social reforms, such as the battle against discrimination, hunger, poor housing, and so on? Many have this concern.

12. A misinterpretation of self-responsibility. Not just a few of the wellness concept's biggest boosters expressed worry about the "double-edged sword" qualities of the philosophy. The idea in this case is that yes, you can make a difference by the choices you make, but some have a far better chance to make good choices than others. This hinder factor often led to the respondent underscoring his or her belief in the significance of attending to the cultures or environments that even the best intentioned individual has to understand and overcome.

13. The long-term payoffs of wellness. Though I personally believe the payoffs of a wellness lifestyle are immediate in some cases and near-term in others, not everyone shared this point of view. Many thought that a definite hindrance to the rapid dissemination of the idea and its widespread adoption would be the fact that the major payoffs (e.g., living longer, disease avoidance, delay of senescence, and the rest) were too far off on the horizon. Most people who need wellness are conditioned to short-range gratifications, other things being the same. (Other things are not the same, of course, but this is not evident to vast numbers of our fellows and sisters.)

14. Relaxation of environmental controls. A biggie. The spread of toxic wastes, even from other than the "unthinkable" (nuclear war) could have devastating effects on the prospects for optimal health.

15. Media advertising for lifestyle vices. A lost of respondents expressed the thought that we tend to underestimate the power of the advertisers to mold public behavior. The relative strengths of all spending for health education versus that which is spent on cigarettes and beer alone was often cited in making this point.

16. The "Jim Fixx backlash" effect. A jogging enthusiast and promoter dies of a heart attack at age 52 while running, ergo, running and other vigorous exercises must be dangerous. Balderdash, of course, but the event and others like it (fitness gurus are mortal) constitute a convenient basis for self delusion for many desirous of same.

17. The "Solomon attention-getter" syndrome. The media is more likely to notice and promote an argument that the world is flat, the Soviets are humanitarians, or exercise does not make you healthy than claims to the opposite, which most assume to be true. This syndrome takes its name from a cardiologist who derived considerable exposure by calling those who exercise rigorously "zealots" and claiming that sedentary living carries small risks.

Which raises another, broader question: Will the wellness movement survive a book, movie, or research report linking health promotion with the Devil, smearing it as a Commie plot, or suggesting that it causes hairy palms?

Almost surely. Still, it will help if wellness promoters and leaders keep their sense of humor—there will be more ludicrous assertions than these in the years to come. As Sir Isaac Newton observed quite a few years ago: "For every action there is an equal and opposite reaction." You have not seen anything yet—just wait until the movement really gets underway and captures the public's imagination. There will be "Low Level Worseness Clubs" all over the land, struggling to perpetuate the old, discredited ways. To no avail, we should hope.

Of course, this commentary should not be interpreted to imply that wellness conference participants are pessimistic about the prospects in the years ahead. These people were encouraged to think of barriers or hindrances to the spread of the wellness concept as an exercise of creative anticipation of worst-case scenarios. A reading of the responses demonstrates that ebullience and optimism rather than gloom and doom marks the expectations of this (regrettably) non-representative sector of the population.

A more typical comment was that of Madeleine Chandler from the School of Nursing at the University of Virginia. She suggested that wellness principles will soon be "taught to preschoolers and children in elementary grades, and become a way of life from childhood."

Others wrote comments to the effect that doctors are already changing their practices to add health screenings and assessments with the help of computers. In the near future, they will be leading teams of health professionals, including wellness counselors, in providing encouragement and support to a public desirous of wellness assistance. One conference participant indicated that "it is the thing of the future—medicine as it has been practiced is a failure. It is true that people are living longer (not due to medical advances) but they are not necessarily living better or more enjoyably. Unless we want to continue to fill the nursing homes with the elderly infirm, we will have to keep them healthy as well as alive. And since 'we' can not do that, we need to have a society that motivates 'them' to do it for themselves." The author of those lines is a physician public health director.

George Pfeiffer, President of the Association for Fitness in Business, told a gathering at the National Wellness Conference at Stevens Point in 1984 that the keys to the future of wellness are flexibility and innovation.

> Corporate wellness is a very young profession. The movement is still very small. But the health of the individual affects the company's health, and vice-versa. Let's view wellness as a strategic benefit—one that protects and enances and/or rehabilitates the company's highest asset—the employee. If we can get that across, the movement will be accelerated.
>
> We need to promote a conceptual model which can be adapted by large and small companies alike. We need to be flexible. If we expect to grow as a profession, we also need to broaden our wares and broaden the means by which these products are delivered.

On a lighter but no less valued note, keynoter Matt Weinstein linked wellness with play and raised self esteem and offered this advice:

> Don't worry. Be happy. Develop a case of 'inverse paranoia,' believing that people are out to do you good. Someday you are going to look back on your life and have a good laugh. Why wait?

Finally, Judy Chiswell of Ohio captured the mood of many participants who took time to reflect on conditions that will enhance the wellness movement:

> The overriding trend is toward a greater awareness of our personal power for change and the greater need for us to take a larger role in our life quality assurance. We are coming to this position in part through a fuller understanding of the interplay of the body/mind/and spirit as we accelerate toward higher levels of humanity. We all have a lot of work ahead of us. I believe it is essential to model the positive effects of wellness without judgment of ourselves or others to demonstrate the integrity, radiance, and love of life we were all meant to enjoy, and that our greatest gift is choice.

Of course, wellness advocates do not get gloomy about all this. Recognition and classification can lead to preparedness.

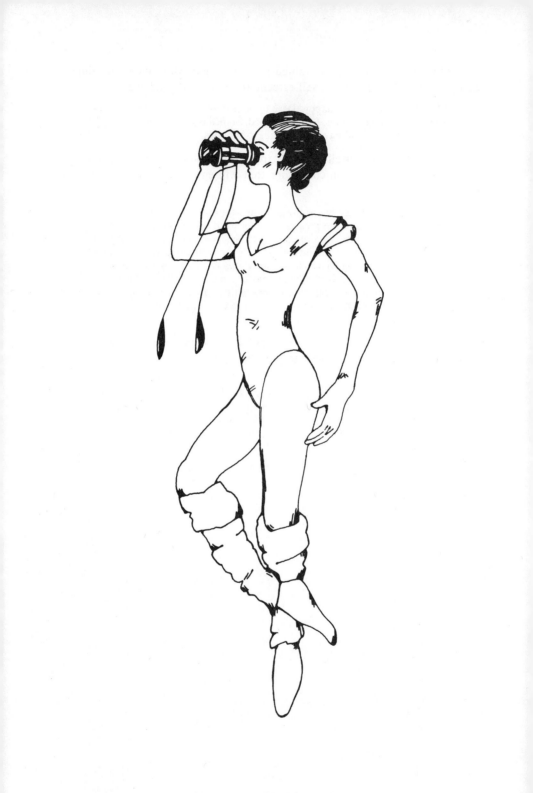

FIVE
Summing Up and Looking Ahead

The Prospects for Wellness

Given such trends and challenges, how might one feel about the prospects for wellness? Several of the "experts" polled had comments about the significance of wellness to date or its future prospects that seemed consistent with the view of this observer.

Alan Dever, Director of Health Service Analysis of Stone Mountain, Georgia, offered a prediction:

> I predict that by the late 1990s we will have approximately 65% to 70% of the U.S. population involved in some form of wellness. I look forward to that time with great anticipation. To be sure, wellness is a concept whose time has come. The responsibility for health is about to be realized by the major population.

Trevor Hancock, Associate Medical Officer at the Toronto Department of Public Health and a well-known health systems futurist, is sure the wellness movement:

> . . . will continue to grow, partly because it is a fast growing economic activity, and partly because hospitals will begin to see the eminent economic sense embodied in the approach. This will be helped considerably if it should turn out that we do develop good epidemiological data to support the broad benefit claims made by the wellness movement.

Consistent with the first concern discussed above, Hancock also noted that the movement must:

> . . . grow from being a somewhat individualist-oriented movement towards a recognition that we can only be healthy in a caring and sharing community and with a healthy physical and social environment. Therefore wellness will become oriented at least as much to diagnosing the state of health of the local community, and the promotion of community wellness rather than merely individual wellness.

Reading the remarks concerning the significance of wellness was the most enjoyable part of the survey.

I think the significance of the movement is that it has reawakened individuals to the realization they, not professionals and large organizations, can be responsible for themselves. It has also made many of us aware we can feel better than "just OK."

Jeffrey Harris, M.D.
Department of Public Health
Tennessee

I also believe the wellness movement has been a very significant trend in American life during the past fifteen years or so—perhaps one of the most important developments during this period. It has been a significant counterbalance to the increasing stress and strains of modern life. It is now beginning to influence the medical community toward great emphasis on health promotion and preventive medicine.

Dr. Walt Schafer
California State University
Chico, California

The significance approaches revolutionary proportions. I see wellness as a superb vehicle for (1) shaping corporate cultures to be more concerned with people and productivity, (2) transforming families from dull, boring, deadly relationships to invigorating, exciting and wonderful support groups, (3) redirecting the focus of students from one-dimensional living, alcoholism and passivity, to wholeness, self-responsibility, and energy development, and (4) creating community cultures that are supportive of positive health and peace.

Rick Bellingham
Former director, Lifegain & Samaritan Health Services
Phoenix, Arizona

We are on the threshold of a historical development in wellness. We are just about to "burst-out" of the innovator or early adopter level and attract a population which does not fit into the traditional medical system.

Dr. Alan Dever

For the future . . . I see nothing but good things. The trend toward self-responsibility in health as in other matters will continue for several years. The intrigue of personal computers will grow rapidly and personal health software will become readily available and frequently used to assess personal health, seek information about health issues, and track health habits. Costs for illness care will not lessen and, therefore, the financial motivation to keep well will be even more obvious than in the past. Employers will take greater and greater interest in the health and well-being of their human resources and will continue to provide health promotion programs at the work-site. *But* . . . there will be those who continue to smoke, overeat and underexercise. And so there will be jobs for health promoters!

Sharon Yenney

The evolving nature of wellness as the movement matures was captured by Lee Amate, a management consultant active in corporate health promotion consulting:

Wellness seminars are going to be quite different in the years to come from today's programs. The dissemination of facts about the basics of fitness/ nutrition/ and stress management will be old hat. Everybody will either know these principles or have enough sense to seek them out when ready to apply them. The new focus will be on contextual wellness issues—how to make work and home life humane and meaningful—and supportive of a healthy existence.

And, my personal favorite of all the responses, this from Don Kemper of Healthwise in Boise, Idaho:

> As a result of the wellness movement there are more smiles, fewer complaints, larger hearts, smaller doctor bills and more satisfied lives.

Well, that may be a little excessive, but it does have a pleasant ring to it. My own view is that wellness is to the health care system what the birth control pill is to our society, namely, an evolutionary leap comparable to the discovery of fire, the shaping of tools, the agrarian revolution, urbanism, advance of the scientific method, and the harnessment of nuclear energy. Of course, I do not enjoy a reputation for excessive moderation or for my tendency to eschew oxymorons. Furthermore, I refer to the potential of the wellness movement; its achievements to date are a bit more modest.

The medical establishment seems to be lining up behind the movement, which is likely to have major consequences for the growth and shaping of the wellness concept in the near future. In a recent special issue of *The Western Journal of Medicine* devoted exclusively to personal health maintenance (December 1984, Volume 141, Number 6), physician Editor Malcolm Watts wrote that the present and obviously growing interest in wellness by business transcends the bottom line of cost and performance.

> People are investing their own time and money in wellness and fitness activities on a scale none of us can remember ever having seen before. . . . It now seems reasonably predictable that as scientific studies in this field continue to be made, wellness and fitness programs will increase in public acceptance, much as has happened with health care in recent decades—and for the same reasons.

In a recent WELLNESS REPORT editorial, I offered a few wild and crazy ideas on future events that may bear reiteration at this point. The subject was a 1985 Vision for Western Civilization that proposed two "heavenly consummations devoutly to be wished" (HCDTBW's), namely:

1. that a vast number of Americans will come out of their closets in 1985 and declare themselves committed to wellness lifestyles
2. that health promotion specialists and others seeking to become so involved will be able to earn a comfortable living providing the inspiration needed by these hundreds of millions who next year acknowledge

Their unconscious wellness tendencies!

The kinds of events which might help to bring all this to fruition are:

1. New skills and techniques for promoting and implementing wellness.

2. Breakthrough research findings on the payoffs of wellness.

3. Accumulation of unassailable data on the benefits of wellness to sponsors.

4. Adoption of the wellness concept by The Great Communicator (i.e., The President).

5. A cultural transformation.

6. A catastrophic rise in medical costs over and above the existing ruinous expense levels.

7. A painful jump in health insurance deductibles payable by employees.

8. A panic inducing disease that strikes sedentary self-abusers who smoke and have no sense of humor.

9. A merger of wellness with a related field (e.g., Employee Assistance Programs) leading to a renaissance of new activities and successes.

10. The adoption of wellness as the fourth R or educational base by all secondary school systems.

11. A magic bullet or cure-all.

Being humble, my self-effusion is tempered by annoying suspicions that I left something out. Try as I may, the missing links elude me, no doubt due to a combination of unfortunate circumstances (e.g., arrogance, loss of brain cells, apathy, excessive drug use, and bad weather).

That is where you come in. But first you have got to get relaxed.

Assume a comfortable position. Play some appropriate music by Mozart or Bach. Close your eyes. Breathe deeply. Progressively relax your muscles. Give yourself hypnotic suggestions about having a slow heart rate, being calm and secure, etc. Visualize being in a serene, fulfilling environment. Get carried away a bit. Now you are ready. For your assignment.

Respond to the above VISION of two HCDTBWs and the list of factors which could help to bring them about. Are the former desirable and/or likely, or neither or both? Is the list complete? (Hint: It is not.) What did I overlook? What is the rank order? Any other remark(s)?

Since this was a participative editorial when it appeared in an earlier Wellness Report, there is no reason it can not be participatory in this incarnation. Feel free to write a response and send it along.

A second editorial looked at the question of quality in wellness education. Again, excerpts should be of interest here:

An Effective Wellness Seminar

There's good news and bad news, folks. The good news is that wellness seminars for employees of business firms are rapidly spreading beyond the 500 Fortune goliaths to thousands of companies with a hundred or fewer workers, and to smaller hospitals and assorted local associations (YMCAs, other fitness clubs, womens' groups, and similar organizations). All this is very good news, indeed.

The bad news is that the content and impact of wellness programs are quite uneven. That is a polite way of saying that some offerings have been known to stink up a place.

It does not take genius, charisma, or uncommon virtue to present a wellness program that entertains, informs, motivates, and enables participants to decide upon, make, and sustain desired behavioral and attitude changes. But it does take preparation and a thorough understanding of the nature and unique qualities of the wellness idea. It also helps to have materials which support a comprehensive approach to the subject, and which encourage participants to involve and commit themselves and their friends and family members to wellness agreements and followup activities.

Anyone personally involved in living a wellness lifestyle can learn how to promote it effectively. Everyone doing so brings something unique and valuable to the task. There is no one and only, tried and true way to present the concept. Furthermore, there's room for lots more people in the business. Even if everyone presently in medical school and all the other health professions suddenly decided to develop careers in health promotion starting tomorrow, we would still have a shortage of wellness teachers lasting at least until the year 2000. Why? Because the level of public awareness and acceptance of even rudimentary principles and techniques for healthy living is so underdeveloped. The vast majority of folks, unlike the "wellest of the well" types who show up at conferences need to hear about wellness as a way out of "middle level mediocrity" health status. That is why we need vast numbers of *additional* wellness promoters, with *varying* educational backgrounds from all culture groups using *diverse* presentation styles. But they must be good in the sense of getting people aroused about their potentials for achieving better health status and giving them the substantive information they need. Furthermore, many people need guides who can impart confidence in their capacity to make it on their own *after* the seminar(s).

Can the measure of seminar effectiveness be defined or otherwise articulated? Can a seminar with "The Right Wellness Stuff" be outlined so wellness promoters can do the job that needs to be done? Will such specificity help those who hire wellness trainers know what to demand and expect?

Of course!

The wellness seminar or training by any name that meets "The Right Stuff" test should have all of the following elements. More are desirable if time and interest levels permit, but these are the basics.

1. Wellness fundamentals, presented in positive, enjoyable to consider, and interactive formulas. The fundamentals include, but are not limited to:

   • The case for personal responsibility. Limits and uses of the health care system, basics of medical self-care, clarification of wellness as distinct from holistic health/prevention/ and health education, and an overview of the extent of and reasons for the wellness movement.

   • The key principles everyone should know regarding nutrition, stress awareness and management, and physical fitness from the perspective not just of disease avoidance and life extension but also the day-to-day advantages of increased human performance.

   • An appreciation for the elements of environmental sensitivity, with an emphasis on the qualities of a truly healthy person in a spiritual/psychological sense. This in addition to helping people discover their "wellness vital signs," which measure how *healthy* rather than how sick they are at the start of a wellness program.

2. A systematic method for getting started. Entails providing participants with an appreciation of what is known about behavior change, what techniques work under which circumstances, and what elements should be included in a comprehensive strategy for setting and accomplishing health goals. Everyone who attends a wellness program should come out better informed and motivated, inspired, *and* equipped with a written plan detailing what he or she expects to do in the coming months to follow up on good intentions. In *Planning for Wellness,** we call this document a personal wellness plan. By whatever name, this systematic device is essential in an effective wellness program.

3. An organized method for getting support. In addition to being well-informed, motivated, and inspired (and in the best of circumstances, entertained, dazzled, awed, sanctified, and saved), quality wellness programs train participants to understand the cultures of which they

*See Ardell, Donald B. and Tager, Mark. *Planning for Wellness: A Guidebook for Optimal Health.* Kendall-Hunt Publishing Company, Dubuque, Ia. 1982.

are a part. When this happens, people can enlist the support of others in changing agreed-upon aspects of their cultures in order to make healthy living both a value and a custom at home, play, and work.

There are other elements presently found in the "good news" wellness programs. No doubt, a great deal more merit will be discovered when all those medical students and other health professionals cut back on their sickness focus and start promoting healthy lifestyles. But for starters, you now understand what to look for when sponsoring a wellness program, and what to provide if you are offering one. In summary, you now know about "The Right Wellness Stuff."

Finally, let's get silly for a moment and imagine four other scenarios, which might be termed "What If?"

What If Scenario Number One

What if the trend toward product accountability were applied by the courts to addictive products? Specifically, what would happen in America if the following scenario were to come about?

Joe Blow, life-long chain smoker, returns from a routine checkup stricken by the news that he has terminal lung cancer. In addition to the usual grieving, fear, depression, and panic, Joe gets mad. He decides to strike back at the R.J. Reynolds Tobacco Company, the makers of Winston, Salem, Camel, and Vantage cigarettes (his former favorites). He decides to claim the company is liable because of deceptive advertisements which led to his addiction, which caused his lung cancer and imminent (and unnecessary) suffering and too-early death. He argues, with the help of able attorneys funded by powerful non-smoking groups, that R.J. Reynolds deceived him by creating the impression in its advertising "that the smoking of cigarettes is a desirable act that can be done safely." Furthermore, Joe alleges that Reynolds advertised that ". . . by smoking so-called low-nicotine cigarettes, that the consumer, including the plaintiff, can reduce any danger to his health; that, in reality, the smoking of low-nicotine cigarettes simply increases the number of cigarettes which the consumer, including plaintiff, is likely to smoke by virtue of his addiction."

Finally, Joe's suit contends that Reynolds should have known smoking of any cigarette is "extremely dangerous" and failed "to point out in its advertising the true extent of the risk involved."

An editorial comment on Joe's suit is in order. While it is true that cigarette ads are deceptive, any moron knows that such ads are less reliable than news in Pravda. What's more, R.J.R.'s products did not cause Joe's disease: Joe did by smoking the damn things. What's more, nobody with even dung for brains believes for a minute that cigarette smoking is "a desirable act that can be done safely," or that low-nicotine versions are any improvement to the noxious weed. Furthermore, Joe's contention that R.J.R. did not point out the true risk is pretty ludicrous. Hell Joe, did you miss the warnings your government forced R.J.R. to put on all those packs you inhaled over the years? So let us realize that Joe is not being bullish on self responsibility with this suit but, considering the target, let us not be querulous.

Wouldn't it be something if some Joe Blow really did that? And why shouldn't he? The World Health Organization has labeled smoking as the largest single treatable cause of death and disability in the world today. The Surgeon General denounced it in 1983 as the chief preventable health hazard in the U.S., holding it responsible for at least 300,000 deaths per year. (In less populous Britain the figure is over 100,000 per year, according to the Royal College of Physicians.*) Dr. John Langdon wrote in the September 1983 OWN Newsletter that the cost to the nation in lost productivity alone is 25 to 30 billion dollars a year. Thus, why shouldn't some Joe Blow sue the makers, promoters, and distributors of this deadly disease-causing vice?

Good news. One Joe Blow is! An AP story out of Indianapolis provided details of this historic action. Imagine if he wins! The implications for wellness are staggering. For one thing, there would be a "gold rush" by entrepreneurs organizing wellness centers to work with millions of poor devils who would either be denied by new laws from continuing their habits or, more likely, convinced at last to get help for their disability before suffering the fate of Joe Blow and 300,000 other Americans (annually). For another, the mortality and morbidity rates would change in a big way, with clear implications for the medical and insurance sectors.

Who knows—perhaps the R.J. Reynolds Tobacco Co. would see fit to design and implement the World's biggest and best wellness center for use by former users of its products and present employees, all of whom might be fruitfully engaged in the production of athletic gear, health foods, and a vast array of other organic and natural goods. All this in the spirit of its having "turned a new leaf." If so, Joe Blow should get the credit.

What if indeed! Is this whistling in the wind? After all, is R.J. Reynolds not the same company that spent $447,000. in 1983 (in vain) trying to defeat an anti-smoking initiative in San Francisco? It is. Are these the same people who are about to start an ad campaign "urging young people not to smoke" (Why am I so suspicious of motives here?) and the rest of us to be courteous to smokers, and vice-versa? The same.

Perhaps the shadow of Joe Blow in the boardroom (presumably smoke-filled) at R.J.R. "lighted" this endeavor. What do you think?

To speed the day of the R.J.R. wellness era, I hereby offer a 50 percent discount on wellness promotion consultation services and seminars for all tobacco company employees, good until the Year 3000 or my death, whichever comes first.

*The Times, "Slowing 'Killing' More Than 100,000 a Year," Nov. 24, 1983, p. 1.

What If Scenario Number Two

What if wonderfully attractive, modestly priced, and capably staffed retreat centers and vacation spas specializing in wellness education were to become readily available to large numbers of businesswomen and men, retired people, church groups, children, and everybody else?

Guess What? This is already happening: let me highlight just one of the best of the genre that I have personally observed and find representative of what we can expect to see in all parts of the country in the years to come.

Steiner-Bell Health Promotion Institute

Located about ten miles from Gatlinburg, Tennessee next to the Great Smoky Mountains National Park on thirty secluded acres, the Institute offers "An exciting retreat setting for a healthy family vacation, a unique regional sales or training meeting, or a non-conventional national convention." The views are great, the food is deliberately nutritious (at $15. for three squares),* and the planned activities are abundant. Smoking is considered anti-social (which of course it is), no tv's are on the premises, the air is pure, the streams clear, the 18 hole golf course uncrowded, and the rooms and facilities are rustic and functional.

The Executive Director of Steiner-Bell is Bill Thompson, one of the early wellness promoters and lecturers who has assembled a capable wellness staff and a network of over 200 consultants brought to the Institute on a regular basis for specialized courses. Asked to summarize the philosophy imparted to all who visit the Institute and participate in its varied programs, Bill listed "five keys to whole-person wellness:"

1. Knowing the purpose and meaning of life.
2. Identifying life's joys and pleasures.
3. Accepting responsibility for self-determination.
4. Finding appropriate sources for motivation.
5. Accepting on-going change in life.**

When the Holiday Inns, Sheratons, Hyatts, Hiltons, and other chains start offering wellness seminars and special packages for travellers, then this

---

*Sample breakfast: Baked apples with raisins, homemade bran muffins, scrambled eggs, oatmeal and orange juice. Sample dinner: Fresh mountain trout, brown and wild rice, pickled Brussels sprouts, Steiner-Bell whole wheat rolls, and strawberry cream dessert.

**For information, write the Institute at Route 3 Box 603, Gatlinburg, Tn. 37738 or call (800) 251–2811. (If in Tennessee, the number is 800 451–0852.)

movement will really take off. Until such time and probably thereafter, you might want to check into a wellness retreat for much more than a good night's sleep.

What If Scenario Number Three

What if a Good Fairy came out of nowhere (which is where Good Fairies hang out) and gave everybody a chance to lead effortless and everlastingly satisfying wellness lifestyles? (No, of course it is not going to happen but this is silly-time, remember?) Specifically, what if the Good Fairy visited you? And gave you a chance to . . . well, here is another excerpt from the AR-DELL WELLNESS REPORT.

The Good Fairy's Wellness Challenge

This is the quarterly participative editorial for those of you who enjoy opportunities to exercise your imagination in the quest to save souls for wellness.

Imagine that you are visited by The Good Fairy. (Don't ask why—trust me! Maybe you gave up smoking, lost a pot belly, stopped grinding your teeth, or otherwise impressed the Fairy. Be grateful that the Good Fairy (GF) is with you.)

The GF offers you three minutes of prime time free of commercial interruption. Your challenge is to provide all the people of the Earth with the benefit of your opinion on any topic—providing that it deals in some manner with the subject of wellness.

Naturally you are delighted with this golden chance to proselytize (at no charge) to the entire universe of humanoids. This will be an event unprecedented in all human history. Yes, you can assume the GF will arrange for everyone to have a tv, to understand your language and to tune in when you deliver your message. You can make assumptions like this when dealing with The GF.

(You will notice that I have avoided assigning a gender to the GF. This is a clever ploy to avoid offending humorless feminists and hostile gays.)

The GF will give you as much time as you desire in order to prepare for your appearance. But the GF is a bit diabolical. "It" wants you to go on as soon as possible, since all people everywhere badly need to hear your wellness message. Therefore, The GF throws into the deal another condition. You can take as long as you like to prepare your remarks but for every minute beyond five minutes from the time you read this you must wait a year to give your three minute message! If it takes ten minutes to prepare (beyond the five minute allotted time) you must wait five years to deliver it; if it takes an hour plan to live another 55 years before your big day arrives.

So, that is the challenge. You have nothing to spend or lose—and the entire world to enlighten. In three minutes you can speak about 450 words at a normal conversational rate.

Kindly write out your remarks. If you are pleased with the results, please consider sharing them with the rest of us. Send your three minute oration to yours truly and, if it is astonishingly profound, dumb, or ridiculous I'll print it for the entertainment of others who read the REPORT.

It is well to be prepared, for one never knows when she or he may be visited by a good fairy.

No self-respecting publisher with chutzpah should ask a reader to consider such a thing as this wellness challenge without leading the way. This I will be happy to do because it just happens that I was visited by the Good Fairy and offered the same deal just described. Here is what I plan to say on universal tv:

> Hi out there everybody. Wow! Isn't this amazing? Imagine: three minutes to address all the inhabitants of Earth. Hope I don't blow it. Hope you like me. Hope I say something sensible. Maybe even useful to you.
>
> A few introductory words about who am I may be of interest. Maybe not. Just a few.
>
> My name is Don. I live in the U.S., close to a city called San Francisco. It is a nice place. I am healthy, still almost young, and I enjoy many conveniences and blessings which many of you, regrettably, do not. I have two children who are growing up free from the ravages of such threats to life and health as famine, pestilence, plague, attacks from hostile neighbors, and the wrath of mean-spirited gods and devils. You might conclude that I am one lucky guy. Then again, if you knew me, you might not. All depends. (That's just a little joke.)
>
> Chances are overwhelming that we have not met and never will. There is just too little time, too much space, too little interest, and too many people. Not to mention so many other, better things to do!
>
> Well, time is running out so I should get to the point. The Good Fairy gave me three minutes to expound on wellness, and I have used more than one of them already. Without saying anything! Truth is, I do not know for sure what I am going to say, but you can probably tell that I'm leading up to it.
>
> Imagine if Jefferson had had this opportunity. Or Lincoln. Or Twain, Shakespeare, or Woody Allen. Alas, you get me. Who can fathom the ways of the Good Fairy?
>
> Alright! I will not waste (more) precious time. This does not happen everyday. Here is my message.
>
> You are *not* responsible for your sex! (Wait, don't leave. It gets better.) You are *not* responsible for your age. Or for the language you speak, the country to which you swear allegiance, the god(s) you were trained to love, serve, and/or fear, if any. You are *not* responsible for the problems of the Universe—or the good things about it, either. You should *not* take yourself too seriously. (You should not take yourself too unseriously, either.)
>
> You *are* responsible for shaping to the maximum extent the fate that awaits you; you *are* responsible for the quality of your existence. The

You *are* responsible for shaping to the maximum extent the fate that awaits you; you *are* responsible for the quality of your existence. The Universe does not care what happens to you. The rocks don't care, the oceans don't care, the air don't care, the sun and moon don't care, and the creatures great and small on sea and land don't care. Except in a philosophical sense that will not affect you, the rest of the human race of about 4.5 billion people do not care, with a handful of exceptions.

So, where does this leave you? If all that I say is true, what should you conclude from this?

Consider this. You are on your own. It pays to care, yourself. Since neither the Universe nor most of its inhabitants will care or get involved in your fate, *you* ought to do so. Wherever you are, whatever your circumstances, actively care for your own well being. Look into the ideas associated with the concept of wellness that the Good Fairy wants me to talk about. This concept of wellness is not a panacea, but it is a big help. It will increase your chances to avoid disease, reduce illness, and live longer. More important, it will promote your prospects of enjoying significant relationships, of having fun in life and in coming to terms with your reasons for living. Do what *you* can to make your life consequential to you, and don't waste a lot of time blaming others, being angry, or sacrificing your own needs for a cause or ideal unless you get a great charge out of doing so.

Be as much of a force as you can but know that greatness is equivocal, justice elusive, success complex, and chance persistent. Consider that everything that happens to you is an opportunity to learn something that will make your life better.

Finally, be sure to love yourself as much as possible, even if you are not convinced that you deserve it.

Love as many others as you can, too. Loving and serving others is one of the surest ways to love and serve yourself.

Well, time is up. Hope the Good Fairy visits many of you, because I would like to hear your messages. May your favorite god bless you, may your weather be pleasant, and may you and all of us enjoy peace and prosperity, purpose and pleasure, and plentiful love.

Be well.

Postscript

Naturally I realize that some aspects of my remarks may be objectionable to persons of Buddhist, Catholic, Jewish, and Protestant persuasions and traditions. Furthermore, I know that Christian and Moslem fundamentalists, moderates and liberals may also find aspects of my thinking to be offensive. Well, what the heck, I can't please everybody.

What IF Scenario Number Four

What if the wellness movement brought about a new and viable forum for public participation in the allocation of scarce resources for health purposes? What if the growing consciousness about personal responsibility, medical wastes, and the neglect of health education in the inner cities led to a citizens revolt against expensive experiments to extend life at the margins? What if the public became truly convinced that handgun controls, mandatory seat belt legislation, the elimination of alcohol and tobacco advertising in any form, and the promotion of fitness and sound dietary practices would do more for the Nation's health than anything achieved by nearly limitless spending on medical technologies?

Sounds interesting? If so, then you are ready for What if scenario number four.

Why Wellness Promoters Will Someday Challenge the Medical Technologists

America desperately needs such a forum. If you have any doubts on this score, just consider two programs or procedures that currently consume a hefty share of taxpayer resources—end stage renal disease treatment and heart transplants.

End stage renal disease treatment is a "downstream" investment, meaning that it is designed to address a problem that exists, not to prevent one from occurring. (For the full analogy, refer to "A Contemporary Fable: Upstream/Downstream" in *High Level Wellness: An Alternative to Doctors, Drugs, and Disease,* Bantam Books, N.Y., 1979, pp. 189–190.) This Federal program serves less than 0.25 percent of all Medicare (Part B) beneficiaries— but eats up ten percent of Medicare expenditures. Who decided this one problem was worth a tenth of all funds available for Medicare? The Congress and the Administration in office at the time, of course, but was the forum as open as it should or could have been? How good was the information available to these decision makers? Perhaps not very: according to one account (*Time,* December 10, 1984, p. 72) Congress expected to pay $140 million for five to seven thousand dialysis patients annually. The first year's tab was $241 million for 10,300 patients. (If you were off in projecting your household budget by a similar percentage, you would be in big trouble. In fact, you would probably go to jail!) Ten years later, the number of customers had jumped to 82,000— and the tab came to two billion dollars a year—and climbing! How did and how does the decision get made to continue spending at this level? Have you ever heard wellness promoters addressing the issue? Keep listening—that day is nearly here (at least according to this What if scenario).

This is just one example of technology and special interests over-powering existing social and political mechanisms for democratic policy making. Let's look at another.

One of the most famous men in America at the start of 1985 was William Schroeder, age 52. A nice man, no doubt, but the basis of his fame represents another example of how vast amounts of limited resources get spent at this time in the absence of a forum for public participation in crucial allocation decisions. If heart replacements are to be available for approximately

50,000 others who need them, the cost will be somewhere between twenty and forty billion dollars annually! Are you ready for that?

Dr. Lewis Thomas, author of *The Lives of a Cell* and President Emeritus of a cancer center, isn't. He is quoted in the above noted *Time* story as believing that this procedure represents an "insupportably expensive, ethically puzzling halfway technology." Others say we must temper our ambitions—and accept the inevitability of disease and death, that such high-tech medicine is a "Faustian bargain" wherein we buy a few days of life at a cost that will bankrupt the Nation. Governor Richard Lamm of Colorado goes farther or at least states it more bluntly: "We have a duty to die and get out of the way with all of our machines and artificial hearts in order that our kids can build a reasonable life." In short, somebody has to pay—and that somebody, naturally, is everybody.

And therein lies the opportunity and the mission for the wellness promoter, supporter, and practitioner. Why not take a lead role in the challenge to work out ways that encourage the public to demand the franchise it deserves, that is, a vote on how health dollars get allocated.

A few decades ago, these kinds of issues did not exist for two reasons: 1) people died quickly from infectious diseases (e.g., influenza and pneumonia) instead of dying slowly from degenerative disorders (heart disease, cancer); and 2) current technologies were neither available nor imagined.

Is this kind of controversy not a wellness issue? Of course it is—and in the years to come wellness promoters better talk about it and delegate the food groups, target heart rate computations, visualization techniques and the like to others or neither they nor the movement will be taken seriously.

According to this fourth and final scenario—such a wellness dialogue will, in fact has already, begun to be heard and will gather momentum rapidly in the months to come.

And someday soon we may decide to spend our health dollars on investments that provide much higher health status returns.

Be a part of it. Think about the issues, gather the facts, prepare the case your way, and help build a forum that will make the wellness perspective a consideration in the allocation of megabucks where they can do the most good for America and its people.

Similar to these two visions were two brief scenarios for the Year 2050—assuming health-enhancing norms as the reality sixty-five years into the future.

A Fearless Prognostication: Health Norms in 2050

Though prognostications, forecasts, and predictions are always hazardous, especially with respect to the future, this should not intimidate the reckless, the arrogant, or the wackos among us from trying their hands at it. In this spirit, let's consider a fearless forecast, a profound prognostication, and a prescient prediction. Perhaps these vignettes will stimulate you to offer a different or extended view of medical care norms in the year 2050. Let us assume that by the year 2050, wellness will be ingrained in our society as both a personal benefit and a social obligation. So, what can we expect?

The scene: a beautiful pastoral setting. Old folks, cheerful but slowed, yours truly among them, make their way to a Wellness Exit Center. Once there, they are inundated with sensory pleasures and/or an atmosphere of melancholia/love or a combination thereof, at the individual's choosing. A skilled, caring staff of wellness facilitators (whose talents blend what in the old days were separate professions of doctor/priest/masseuse/counselor/and geisha) minister to the guests, who have come of their own volition because their life forces are not acceptable to them any longer. When sleep comes, there is no grief.

Another scene: a fine restaurant. The menu offers extraordinarily tempting delicacies, all of which are very high in nutrients by today's standards because the patrons would have nothing less. A stranger enters, dressed in the garb of the 1980's. Seems the fellow has been in a time warp. He expresses dismay at the choices and is not at all pleased to learn that the only "hamburger" known to exist is at the exhibition of "Yesterday's World" at the Epcot Center in Orlando. He lights a cigarette and quickly inhales a deep breath of the smoke and gases before he realizes that several of the women are screaming and others are rushing toward him to give assistance. In a flash, he is overwhelmed and given respiration.

Within 30 seconds, an electric-powered wellness enhancement vehicle has arrived. He is taken off, amid a wail of sirens and flashing lights, to a life-appreciation center where he will get assistance for whatever disturbances and imbalances caused him to jeopardize his life and the health of others by a lewd and perverted, anti-social, and suicidal act of smoking a cigarette—in a public place at that! An investigation by the Commission to Interdict Aggression (CIA) is instituted to discover where he got the noxious weed, which has been outlawed since the turn of the last century.

Send your visions and hallucinations concerning how things will be in 2050 to the AWR; all entries are welcomed, so long as they are in accord with my view of things. See you, someday, at the Exit Center. Be well— or else.

A bright future for wellness was signalled in late 1984 when the United Auto Workers and General Motors concluded negotiations on a new contract which included a provision for wellness benefits. (See *Newsweek,* November 5, 1984, pp. 96–97.) The recognition of wellness as a valued union benefit marks a watershed indicator which *Newsweek* termed a milestone: namely, wellness as a new item on "the roster of inalienable American rights."

At the end of a lecture on the history and future of wellness at the National Wellness Conference in 1984, I invited a few of my friends whom I felt were doing important work in the field to offer their summary thoughts on the future of this movement. Here are excerpts from their remarks.

I think the establishment (i.e., big business and the "illness makers" like the alcohol and tobacco industries) is listening very carefully to wellness. I'm very optimistic about the directions underway.

Dennis Elsenrath

It's very important that we work with the shapers of the next generations. Let's get teachers excited about their lives—and they will figure ways to get the message to the kids.

William Hettler

I believe the future of the wellness movement is in dealing with young people in such a way that the wellness philosophy is an integral, natural growing process for them, not rules set down in isolation.

Sandy Queen

We are novices at helping people to experience wellness—years from now we will have a whole range of new ways to get people involved. We need to help each other more. I think a key is to encourage people to become teachers—because the people who change the most are those who teach wellness.

Donald A. Tubesing

Once we have attended to the basic dimensions of fitness, nutrition, and stress management, we are going to turn to the spiritual realm, raise our consciousness, and learn to live in harmony with each other and the planet. As we learn to feel better about ourselves, we will then be able to reach out to others and tap into long forgotten roots.

Jan Berry Schroeder

One area that is so important is discovering the power of the brain in our own healing and in the common energy system we share with all mankind. I hope wellness groups will cooperate and not be competitive. Let's share what we have and not carve out turfs because cooperation is our salvation and the soul of the future. I believe we will survive because of wellness people.

Elaine Sullivan

Our own self perception of our influence lags behind the impact we are having—we come together and change in ways not evident to us. Each of us will keep this movement going in our own communities, networks, and families.

Through wellness, we will eventually get in touch with the larger world family and establish a greater harmony with nature. At that time our prospects for overcoming hunger, pollution, and the threat of war will be brighter. If we do not do this, we won't be here—and if we are not here we can't be well.

Fred Leafgren

The future of wellness will be shaped in large part by our ability to create a sound cultural environment which encourages more positive and informed choices. As adults, we can help by modeling the behaviors and benefits of wellness in order that young people have a better picture of how to build strong self-images—the key building block for a wellness lifestyle.

Chuck Hess

Conclusion

"Wellness is neither a pipedream nor a panacea," as Willis Goldbeck, President of the Washington Business Group on Health recently observed.[81] By itself, this is surely so: it is not the solution. On the other hand, it is clear that there can be no solution(s) to our national health problems without it. Wellness is, as much as anything else, an opportunity, perhaps the best opportunity we have had—both as a society and as individuals. Let us not miss it.

Above all, let us remember that the history of wellness has not been written, yet. This accounting is not even a preface for what is to come. "The future," as Parkinson has reminded us, "lies ahead." This movement is for real. The promise for each of us is highly attractive—and exciting. We might begin to ask ourselves questions such as: How can we support each other in doing better work and how can we most expeditiously address the concerns defined in this short review of the movement's history?

The message bears repeating one more time: the history of wellness is still to be written because it has not occurred, as yet. You can be among the authors of such a history by the roles you play. Be bold—therein lies the power, genius, and magic about which Goethe wrote. As a modern Delphi Oracle might observe about the life of the wellness concept, this wonderful fad/movement/craze we want to last forever: "Its life is truly in your hands."

Keep your sense of humor. Safeguard your balance. Be good to each other. And, be well.

NOTES

1. Ardell, Donald B. *High Level Wellness: An Alternative to Doctors, Drugs and Disease* (Emmaus, PA: Rodale Press, 1977, and New York, NY: Bantam Books, 1979); _____ , *14 Days to a Wellness Lifestyle* (Mill Valley, CA: Whatever Publishing, 1982); _____ and Mark J. Tager, *Planning for Wellness* (Dubuque, IA: Kendall/Hunt Publishing Co., 1982). Also, Center for Social Welfare Research, School of Social Work, Univ. of Washington, *The Wallingford Wellness Project—An Innovative Health Promotion Program with Older Adults* (Seattle, WA, 1982); Clark, Carolyn Chambers, *Enhancing Wellness: A Guide for Self-Care* (New York, NY: Springer Publishing Co., 1981); S. Kammermann, K. Doyle, R. Valois, S. Cox, *Wellness R.S.V.P.* (Menlo Park, CA: Benjamin/Cummings Publishings Co., 1982); McDowell, C. Forrest. *Leisure Wellness: Concepts & Helping Strategies.* Eugene Oregon: SunMoon Press, 1983; Popenoe, Cris, *Wellness* (Washington, DC: Yes! Inc., 1977); Schafer, Walt, *Wellness Through Stress Management* (Davis, CA: International Dialogue Press, 1983); R. S. Ryan and J. W. Travis, *The Wellness Workbook* Berkeley, CA.: Ten Speed Press) 1981; and Ziebell, Beth, *Wellness: An Arthritis Reality* (Dubuque, IA: Kendall/Hunt Publishing Co., 1981).

2. The National Wellness Conference is sponsored by the Institute for Lifestyle Improvement, University of Wisconsin–Stevens Point, Stevens Point, WI 54481.

3. The Center for Health Promotion of the American Hospital Association, 840 North Lake Shore Drive, Chicago, Illinois 60611 maintains an up-to-date list of hospital-based wellness centers and offers a booklet entitled "Planning Hospital and Health Promotion Services for Business and Industry." Another excellent source of information about hospital-based wellness centers is The National Center for Health Promotion, 3772 Plaza Drive, Suite 5, Ann Arbor, Mi. 48104.

4. Dunn, Halbert L. *High Level Wellness.* Arlington, Va.: R.W. Beatty, 1961.

5. *The American Heritage Dictionary of the English Language.* Houghton-Mifflin Co.: New York, 1982, p. 482; *Webster's New World Dictionary.* Warner Books: New York, 1979, p. 220; and *The Merriam Webster Dictionary,* Pocket Books: New York, p. 258.

6. Foege, William H. "Guest Commentary: Health Education—A Challenge for the Future," *Health Education Focal Points.* U.S. Dept. of Health and Human Services, Public Health Service, July, 1983, p. 1.

7. For mass market magazine versions of the wellness dimensions and philosophy, see "The Wellness Lifestyle for a Dynamic Future," *Bestways,* March, 1983, pp. 56–63, and "The Wellness Revolution," *Health Picture Magazine,* Spring, 1982, pp. 23–27.

8. For information about the Institute and its varied wellness programs, write Joseph Opatz, Director, Institute for Lifestyle Improvement, Delzell Hall, University of Wisconsin–Stevens Point, Stevens Point, WI. 54481.

9. For information write the Institute Director at Tempe Wick Road, Morristown, NJ. 07960.

10. LaLonde, Marc. *A New Perspective on the Health of Canadians.* Ottawa: Government of Canada, 1974.

11. Ardell, Donald B., Leister, D. Wesley, and Martin, Susan M. "Wellness Promotion: A Proposed Focus for Regional Planning in Canada," *Canadian Journal of Public Health,* September/October, 1980, Vol. 71, pp. 299–303.

12. Senate Select Committee on Nutrition and Human Needs. George McGovern, Chairperson. *Dietary Goals for the United States.* Washington, D.C.: U.S. Government Printing Office, 1977. (Publication no. 052-070-03913-2).

13. For a copy, write the Center for Health Promotion, AHA, 840 North Lake Shore Drive, Chicago, ILL 60611.

14. Public Health Service. *Healthy People. The Surgeon General's Report on Health Promotion and Disease Prevention.* U.S. Dept. of Health, Education, and Welfare. Superintendent of Documents, U.S. Government Printing Office, 1979.

15. Hedberg, Augustin. "Health Care: Getting the Best Value." *Mony Magazine.* September, 1982. pp. 55–58. Also, Ardell, Donald B. "A Wellness Model For National Health Insurance," *Journal of Health and Human Resources Administration,* Vol. 5, No. 3, Winter, 1983, pp. 321–333.

16. For more information about Stay Well, write for a brochure "Health Incentive Plan" from Blue Shield of Northern California at P.O. Box 7136, San Francisco, CA 94120.

17. Knowles, John (Ed.). *Doing Better and Feeling Worse: Health in the U.S.* New York: W.W. Norton, 1977. Also in Daedalus, Winter, 1977. 106 (1).

18. Blue Cross Association, The Rockefeller Foundation, and the Health Policy Program at the University of California (San Francisco). *The Proceedings of the Conference on Future Directions in Health Care: The Dimensions of Medicine.* Chicago: Blue Cross Association.

19. One of the better sources for books and articles about alternative strategies for cost control is *Health for the Whole Person,* Edited by Arthur Hastings, James Fadiman, and James Gordon. New York: Bantam Books, 1981.

20. Ferguson, Tom. *Medical Self Care: Access to Health Tools.* P.O. Box 717, Inverness, CA 94937.

21. Toffler, Alan. *The Third Wave.* New York: Bantam, 1981.

22. Pilch, John. *Wellness: Your Invitation To A Full Life.* Minneapolis: Winston Press, 1981.

23. Cousins, Norman. *Anatomy of an Illness.* New York: Bantam, 1979.

24. Maslow, Abraham. *The Psychology of Science.* Chicago: Henry Regnery, 1966.

25. Rogers, Carl. *Becoming Partners.* New York: Delacorte Press, 1972.

26. Watts, Alan. *Nature, Man, and Woman.* New York: Pantheon, 1958, and _____ . *The Book: On the Taboo Against Knowing Who You Are.* New York: Vintage, 1966.

27. Leonard, George. *The Transformation*. Los Angeles: J.P. Tarcher, 1981.

28. Capra, Fritjof. *The Tao of Physics*. Berkeley, CA: Shambhala, 1975.

29. *Proceedings of the National Conference on Health Promotion Programs in Occupational Settings: State of the Art Papers,* Washington, D.C.: Office of Health Information and Health Promotion, Public Health Service, DHEW, January, 1979; and Sehnert, Keith W. and Tillotson, John K. *A National Health Care Strategy: How Business Can Promote Good Health for Employees and Their Families.* Washington, D.C.: The National Chamber Foundation, 1978.

30. Two excellent sources are the Washington Business Group for Health, 922 Pennsylvania Avenue S.W., Washington, D.C. 20003, and the U.S. Chamber of Commerce, 1615 H. Street N.W., Washington, D.C. 20201.

31. See "Health Strategy for Ontario: Wellness, Environment, and Sickcare," *Paradigm Health*. Toronto: Institute for Alternative Futures, 1983.

32. For details about this innovative industry effort, write Scherer Brothers Lumber Company at Mississippi River and 9th Avenue Northeast, Minneapolis, Minn. 55413. Also, refer to any of the following:

    Fielding, Jonathan E., and Breslow, Lester. "Health Promotion Programs Sponsored by California Employers," 1983

    American Journal of Public Health, May 1983, Vol. 73, No. 5.; and "Effectiveness of Employee Health Improvement Programs" *Journal of Occupational Medicine,* Vol. 23, No. 11, November 1982;

    Green, Lawrence W., Dr. P. H., "How to Evaluate Health Promotion," *Hospitals,* October 1, 1979;

    "Health Capitalist Systems," *INC.,* November, 1983, p. 172; Healthworks Northwest (601 Valley St., Seattle, Wa. 98109) has produced several booklets which may be of help to wellness program organizers, including "Employee Health Promotion: A Guide For Starting Programs at the Workplace" ($15), "Health Promotion Programs in Small Businesses," "Guidelines for Selecting Health Promotion Providers," and "Needs Assessment Manual."

    Goldberg, Rob. "Working Out At Work," *Savvy,* December 1983, pp. 54–59.;

    Managing Health Promotion in the Workplace Guidelines for Implementation and Evaluation, Rebecca S. Parkinson and Associates, Mayfield Publishing Company, 1982;

    McManus, Kevin. "Forced Wellness?" *Forbes,* Nov. 7, 1983.

    Wellness At Work: A Report on Health and Fitness Programs for Employees of Business and Industry, Robert M. Cunningham, Jr., An Inquiry Book, 1982.

33. Illich, Ivan. *Medical Nemesis*. New York, NY: Pantheon Books, 1976.

34. Carlson, Rick. *End of Medicine*. New York: Wiley-Interscience, 1975.

35. Mendelsohn, Robert. *Confessions of a Medical Heretic*. Chicago, IL: Contemporary Books, 1979.

36. Dubos, René. *Mirage of Health*. New York, NY: Harper & Row, Publishers, Inc., 1959.

37. Browne, Harry. *How I Found Freedom in an Unfree World*. New York: Avon, 1973.

38. Leonard, Jon (et.al.). *Live Longer Now: The First One Hundred Years of Your Life.* New York: Grosset and Dunlap, 1974, and Pritikin, Nathan. *The Pritikin Program for Diet and Exercise.* New York: Grosset & Dunlap, 1979.

39. Lappé, Frances Moore. *Diet for a Small Planet.* New York: Ballentine, 1975.

40. Cheraskin, E. (et.al.). *Psychodietetics.* New York: Bantam, 1976; and *Diet and Disease.* New Canaan, Conn.: Keats, 1977.

41. Cooper, Kenneth H. *Aerobics.* New York: Bantam, 1968; _____ . *The Aerobics Way.* New York: Evans and Company, 1977.

42. Sheehan, George. *Dr. Sheehan on Running.* Mountain View, CA: World, 1975.

43. Bailey, Covert. *Fit or Fat.* Boston: Houghton-Mifflin, 1978.

44. Selye, Hans. *Stress Without Distress.* New York: Signet, 1974.

45. Benson, Herbert. *The Relaxation Response.* New York: Avon, 1975.

46. Pelletier, Kenneth R. *Mind as Healer, Mind as Slayer: A Holistic Approach to Preventing Stress Disorders.* New York: Delta, 1977.

47. Vickery, Donald M. *Life Plan For Your Health.* Reading, MA: Addison-Wesley, 1978; and, _____ . *Take Care of Yourself: A Consumer Guide to Medical Care.* Reading, MA: Addison-Wesley, 1980.

48. Samuels, Michael and Bennett, Hal. *The Well Body Book.* New York: Random House/Book Works, 1973.

49. Sehnert, Keith. *How to be Your Own Doctor (Sometimes).* New York, Grosset and Dunlap, 1975.

50. Ferguson, Tom. *Medical Self-Care: Access to Self-Help Tools.* New York: Simon and Schuster, 1980.

51. Kemper, Donald (et.al.). *Healthwise Handbook.* Garden City, NY: Doubleday & Co., Inc., 1979.

52. Belloc, Nedra and Breslow, L. "Relationship of Physical Health Status and Health Practice," *Preventive Medicine,* 1972, 1, 409–421.

53. Paffenbarger, R. S. Jr. and Hale, W. "Work Activity and Coronary Heart Disease," *New England Journal of Medicine,* 1976. 292, 545–550.

54. See Institute of Medicine. *Perspectives on Health Promotion and Disease Prevention in the U.S..* Washington, D.C.: National Academy of Sciences, January, 1978. Also, see Robbins, L. C. and Hall, J. H. *How to Practice Prospective Medicine.* Indianapolis, In.: Methodist Hospital, 1979; and Hall, J. H. and Zwemer, J. D. *Prospective Medicine.* Indianapolis, In.: Methodist Hospital, 1979.

55. Surgeon General's Report on Smoking and Health, Department of Health and Human Services, Washington, D.C.

56. Kass, Leon R. "Regarding the End of Medicine and the Pursuit of Health," *The Public Interest,* 40 (Summer 1975).

57. Mckeown, Thomas. *The Role of Medicine: Dream, Mirage, or Nemesis?* London: Rock Carling Fellowship, Nuffield Provincial Hospital Trust. 1976.

58. Fuchs, Victor. *Who Shall Live? Health Economics and Social Change.* New York: Basic Books, 1974.

59. Michael Foucault, *Madness and Civilization* (New York, 1967); Eliot Fredison, *Professional Dominance* (Chicago, 1970); Erving Goffman, *Asylums* (New York, 1961); R. D. Laing, *The Politics of Experience* (New York, 1967); Thomas J. Schneff, *Being Mentally Ill* (Chicago, 1966); Thomas S. Szasz, *The Myth of Mental Illness* (New York, 1961); and Howard D. Waitzkin and Barbara Waterman, *The Exploitation of Illness in Capitalist Society* (Indianapolis, 1974).

60. Dunn. *Op.Cit.*

61. Ardell, Donald B. "Meet John Travis, Doctor of Well Being," *Prevention,* April, 1975, pp. 62–69; and Leonard, George. "The Holistic Health Revolution," *New West Magazine,* May, 1976.

62. Ryan, Regina Sara and Travis, John. *Wellness Workbook.* Berkeley, CA: Ten Speed Press, 1981.

63. For information about Travis' seminars, newsletter and so on, write Wellness Associates, P.O.Box 5433, Mill Valley, CA 94941.

64. Ardell, Donald B. *High Level Wellness: An Alternative to Doctors, Drugs and Disease.* Rodale Press 1977, Bantam Books 1979.

65. Ardell, *op.cit.* Also (with Carlson, Jon) "Physical Fitness as a Pathway to Wellness and Effective Counseling," *Counseling and Human Development,* Vol. 13, 1981, pp. 1–12.

66. Allen, Robert. *Lifegain.* New York: Appleton-Century-Crofts, 1981. To contact Dr. Allen, write The Human Resources Institute, Tempe Wick Road, Morristown, N.J. 07960.

67. For information, write to Frost Valley, % Wellness Programs, Frost Valley YMCA, Olivera, NY 12462.

68. Ardell, Donald B. "High Level Wellness at Camp," *Elementary School Guidance and Counseling,* December, 1979, Vol. 14, No. 2, pp. 168–174.

69. Ardell, Donald B. "From Omnibus Tinkering to High Level Wellness: The Movement Toward Holistic Health Planning," *American Journal of Health Planning.* October, 1976, pp. 15–34.

70. ———. "High Level Wellness and the HSA's: A Health Planning Success Story," *American Journal of Health Planning,* July, 1978, pp. 1–18.

71. ——— and Robbins, Leonard. "High Level Wellness and the HSA's: The Failure to Move From Advocacy to Action," *Journal of Health and Human Resources Administration,* May, 1980, pp. 429–448.

72. For information, write to the Center at AHA, 840 North Lake Shore Drive, Chicago, IL 60611.

73. For information, write to the Center at Wellness Systems, 3444 South Emerson Street, Englewood, CO 80110.

74. See Peccei, Aurelio. *One Hundred Pages for the Future.* New York: Mentor, 1981; also Ferguson, Marilyn. *The Aquarian Conspiracy.* Los Angeles: J.P. Tarker, 1980.

75. For a copy of the Trend Report on Health Futures based on a Delphi Study sponsored by the Health Central System, the Naisbitt Group, and the Center for Health Services Research, University of Minnesota, write Pamela Garside, Health Central, 601 Brookdale Towers, 2810 Fifty Seventh Avenue North, Minneapolis, MN 55430.

76. Naisbitt, John. *Megatrends: Ten New Directions Transforming Our Lives.* New York: Warner Books, 1982 and in *Hospital Forum,* July–August, 1983.

77. Bell, Daniel. *The Coming of Post-Industrial Society: A Venture in Social Forecasting.* New York: Basic Books, 1976; and Yankelovich, Daniel. "New Rules in American Life," *Psychology Today,* April, 1981.

78. Ferguson, Tom. Address at the Annual Health Promotion Strategies Conference Stevens Point, WI, on July 19, 1983 entitled "The Third Wave in Health: Wellness and Illness Self Care".

79. Eckhouse, John, "Educational Software Market Boom," *San Francisco Examiner,* July 31, 1983, Section D, p. 1, and Laughlin, Molly. "The Burgeoning Self-Care Industry," *Medical Self-Care,* Fall, 1983, pp. 32–34.

80. The President's Council on Fitness and Sports, Washington, D.C. 20201.

81. Remarks at the First Annual Kaiser Permanente Health Promotion Strategies Conference entitled "New Roles/New Directions," June 28, 1983, Portland, Oregon.

INDEX

Abt Associates, 11
Actualizations, 12
Allen, Robert, 23, 36
Allen, Woody, 63
Amate, Lee, 54–55
American Association of Homes for the
    Aging, 40
American Cancer Society, 16
American Health Planning Association, 14
American Hospital Association, 7, 8, 11, 15,
    27–28
American Lung Association, 15
American Medical Association, 14
American Public Health Association, 14
American Sports Data Research, 45
Ardell Culture Test, 23–24
Arica, 12
Association for Fitness in Business, 14

Bailey, Covert, 12
Bellingham, Rick, 54
Belloc, Nedra, 13
Bennett, Hal, 12
Benson, Herbert, 12
Bertera, Robert, 15
Blue Shield, 7
Bonnie Bell, 11
Breslow, L., 13
Brown, Halbe, 26
Browne, Harry, 12

Canada Life Assurance, 11
Canadian Ministry of Health and Welfare, 6
Capra, Fritjof, 9
Carlson, Rick, 12
Chandler, Madeline, 50
Chapman, Larry, 15
Chase Manhattan Bank, 11
Cheraskin, Emmanuel, 12
Chiswell, Judy, 51
Control Data, 11
Cooper, Kenneth, 12, 15, 45
Cousins, Norman, 9

Dever, Alan, 53, 54
Doing Better and Feeling Worse, 8
Dubois, Rene, 12
Dunn, Halbert L., 2, 22, 26

Elsenrath, Denny, 26, 68
EST, 12

Ferguson, Tom, 9, 12
Fixx, Jim, 49
Fitzgerald, F. Scott, 2
Foege, William, 2
Fonda, Jane, 17
Framingham, 13
Frost Valley YMCA, 26, 40
Fries, James, 12
Fuchs, Victor, 13
Future Directions in Health Care, 8

Goldbeck, Willis, 69
Goldberg, Sheldon, 40
Goethe, 69
Good Fairy (The), 62
Governors' Councils, 28
Griffith, Donald R., 14

Hancock, Trevor, 53
Harris, Jeffrey, 54
Health Systems Agencies, 27
Hess, Chuck, 68
Hettler, Bill, 25, 26, 38, 68
Hubbard Milling, 11

Iacocca, Lee, 48
IBM, xiii, 11
Illich, Ivan, 12
Institute for Lifestyle Improvement, 26